GOODSON MUMBA

From Workforce to Winforce

Strategic HRM in Action

Copyright © 2024 by Goodson Mumba

All rights reserved. No part of this publication may be reproduced, stored or transmitted in any form or by any means, electronic, mechanical, photocopying, recording, scanning, or otherwise without written permission from the publisher. It is illegal to copy this book, post it to a website, or distribute it by any other means without permission.

First edition

ISBN: 9798335616010

This book was professionally typeset on Reedsy.
Find out more at reedsy.com

Contents

Preface ... iv
Acknowledgement ... vi
Dedication ... vii
Disclaimer ... viii
1 Chapter 1: The Catalyst for Change ... 1
2 Chapter 2: Charting the Course ... 20
3 Chapter 3: Developing the Strategy ... 32
4 Chapter 4: Talent Acquisition and Recruitment ... 44
5 Chapter 5: Onboarding and Integration ... 55
6 Chapter 6: Employee Engagement and Retention ... 66
7 Chapter 7: Leadership Development ... 77
8 Chapter 8: Performance Management ... 87
9 Chapter 9: Learning and Development ... 97
10 Chapter 10: Compensation and Benefits ... 107
11 Chapter 11: Organizational Culture and Change Management ... 117
12 Chapter 12: Diversity and Inclusion ... 126
13 Chapter 13: Technology and HR Analytics ... 136
14 Chapter 14: Measuring Success and Continuous Improvement ... 145
15 Chapter 15: Reflections and Future Outlook ... 154
About the Author ... 163

Preface

In the dynamic and ever-evolving landscape of business, the role of Human Resource Management (HRM) has undergone a profound transformation. What was once a function focused primarily on administrative tasks and employee relations has now emerged as a critical driver of organizational success. The strategic integration of HRM into the broader business framework has the potential to transform a traditional workforce into a powerful "Winforce" – a team that is not only efficient and productive but also innovative, agile, and resilient.

The journey detailed in these pages began with recognizing the urgent need for change within TechSolutions. Faced with mounting challenges, from high employee turnover to stagnant growth, it became clear that a fundamental shift was necessary. This book chronicles that transformation, led by Sarah Thompson, the newly appointed Chief Human Resources Officer (CHRO), and the dedicated team that supported her vision.

Through each chapter, we delve into the various facets of strategic HRM, from talent acquisition and onboarding to employee engagement, performance management, and beyond. We explore the importance of aligning HR initiatives with business goals, the power of data-driven decision-making, and the impact of fostering a culture of continuous learning and inclusivity.

Our aim with this book is to provide you, the reader, with

a roadmap for implementing strategic HRM in your own organization. We offer actionable insights, practical tools, and illustrative case studies to guide you through the complexities of transforming your workforce into a Winforce. Whether you are an HR professional, a business leader, or an organizational strategist, you will find valuable perspectives and strategies to elevate your HR practices and drive organizational success.

"From Workforce to Winforce: Strategic HRM in Action" is a testament to the power of visionary leadership, collaborative effort, and unwavering commitment to excellence. It is a story of transformation, resilience, and the relentless pursuit of greatness. As you embark on this journey with us, we hope you are inspired to reimagine the potential of your workforce and harness the power of strategic HRM to achieve extraordinary results.

Thank you for joining us on this transformative journey. Let's turn your workforce into a Winforce.

Warm regards.

Goodson Mumba

Acknowledgement

I would like to eternally and gratefully acknowledge the Almighty God for the infinite intelligence from His universal mind where we draw from all that we come to know and are yet to know. May I also acknowledge and thank everyone that has played a part in my journey of life in terms of spiritual, moral, emotional and material support.

Dedication

I extend my sincerest gratitude to my beloved wife, Edith Mumba, and our children, Angelina, Lubuto, Letticia, Lulumbi, and Butusho, for their unwavering support and understanding throughout the conception, writing, and eventual publication of this book, despite the sacrifices and challenges they endured.

Disclaimer

This book is a work of fiction. Names, characters, businesses, places, events, and incidents are either the products of the author's imagination or used in a fictitious manner. Any resemblance to actual persons, living or dead, or actual events is purely coincidental.

1

Chapter 1: The Catalyst for Change

Overview of TechSolutions' struggles

In the bustling city of Newbridge, TechSolutions, a mid-sized technology company, was teetering on the brink of crisis. Once known for its innovative software solutions, the company was now plagued with high employee turnover, dwindling morale, and stagnating growth. The energy that once filled its modern, glass-walled offices had turned into a palpable tension. Departments that used to collaborate seamlessly were now siloed, with communication breakdowns becoming a daily frustration. Quarterly reports painted a grim picture, showing a steady decline in productivity and market share.

Introduction of Sarah Thompson as CHRO

Against this backdrop of uncertainty, James Parker, the company's forward-thinking yet increasingly desperate CEO, decided to make a bold move. After an extensive search, he hired Sarah Thompson, a dynamic and experienced HR leader renowned for her strategic prowess. Sarah walked into her new role with a reputation for transforming troubled organizations. On her first day, she took a deep breath as she stepped into the TechSolutions building, her mind already buzzing with ideas.

Initial assessment of company challenges

Sarah's first task was to understand the depth of TechSolutions' problems. She spent weeks conducting interviews, reviewing policies, and analyzing data. She spoke with employees across all levels, from the seasoned engineers to the young interns. What she found was a company mired in outdated HR practices, lack of clear career paths, and a pervasive sense of disengagement. Many employees felt their talents were underutilized, and the lack of development opportunities was a common complaint.

Executive team's expectations and skepticism

When Sarah presented her findings to the executive team, the room was filled with a mix of anticipation and skepticism. James Parker, with his greying hair and determined expression, listened intently. He was hopeful but wary; he had seen many initiatives fail to take root. Michael Rivera, the CFO, was particularly vocal in his doubts, questioning the financial viability of Sarah's proposed changes. He was joined by several other executives who were concerned about the disruptions that a major overhaul would cause.

Sarah's vision for strategic HRM

Undeterred by the cautious reception, Sarah laid out her vision. She spoke passionately about transforming TechSolutions' HR from a back-office function to a strategic partner in driving business success. She emphasized the need for a holistic approach that aligned HR initiatives with the company's strategic objectives. Sarah detailed her plan: revamping the recruitment process, implementing a comprehensive onboarding program, fostering a culture of continuous learning, and developing leadership from within.

Setting the stage for transformation

James, recognizing the need for bold action, gave Sarah his full support. He addressed the executive team, underscoring the critical nature of the changes and urging them to embrace the transformation. With the CEO's backing, Sarah began assembling a team of like-minded HR professionals and change agents from within the company. She knew the road ahead would be challenging, filled with resistance and setbacks. But Sarah was resolute, fueled by the belief that TechSolutions could not only recover but thrive.

As she walked out of the boardroom that day, Sarah felt a renewed sense of purpose. The real work was about to begin. The first step was to turn a skeptical workforce into a motivated winforce, ready to reclaim their company's innovative edge.

And with that, the journey of transformation at TechSolutions had truly begun.

Overview of TechSolutions' struggles

TechSolutions was founded in the late 1990s by a group of visionary software engineers. For years, it thrived as a leader in custom software solutions, catering to an impressive roster of clients. The company's office, located in a sleek, glass-fronted building in Newbridge's tech district, was once a hive of innovation and excitement. But in recent years, the spark had faded.

The decline began subtly. A few key employees left for more exciting opportunities at rival firms, their departures barely causing a ripple. But as the months passed, the trickle turned into a flood. Talented developers and managers departed, leaving behind a skeletal crew struggling to keep up with deadlines and client demands. The once vibrant corridors of TechSolutions now echoed with a sense of emptiness and disillusionment.

On a dreary Monday morning, James Parker, the company's CEO, sat in his corner office, staring out at the gray cityscape. The past quarter's financial report lay open on his desk, its numbers bleak and unforgiving. Revenue was down, profits were razor-thin, and the board of directors was growing impatient. James sighed, running a hand through his graying hair. He had led the company through thick and thin, but this time felt different. The problems ran deeper than just a few bad quarters.

Down in the development bullpen, Cynthia Chen, a brilliant software engineer, was losing her motivation. She had joined

CHAPTER 1: THE CATALYST FOR CHANGE

TechSolutions straight out of college, drawn by its reputation for cutting-edge projects and collaborative culture. But now, she found herself drowning in mundane tasks, with little opportunity for growth or innovation. Her once vibrant team was a shadow of its former self, the energy replaced by a resigned acceptance of mediocrity.

Across the office, in the HR department, the situation was equally dire. Michelle, the long-serving HR manager, was overwhelmed. She was juggling exit interviews, recruitment ads, and disgruntled employee complaints, all while trying to keep up with the outdated HR systems. The last employee engagement survey had painted a stark picture: widespread dissatisfaction, lack of career development, and a pervasive feeling that the company no longer cared about its people.

The symptoms of decline were everywhere. Project deadlines were missed with increasing regularity, leading to strained client relationships. In team meetings, discussions were dominated by finger-pointing and frustration rather than problem-solving. Morale was at an all-time low, and productivity had taken a nosedive. The once-proud TechSolutions was now a company adrift, its competitive edge dulled.

James knew something had to change. Desperate for solutions, he began searching for a seasoned HR leader who could turn things around. That's when he came across Sarah Thompson's impressive track record. Her work at other tech firms had earned her a reputation as a strategic HR visionary capable of driving real change.

James wasted no time in reaching out to Sarah. Their first meeting was a turning point. Sarah, with her clear-eyed vision and unwavering confidence, seemed like the answer to TechSolutions' prayers. She spoke about aligning HR with business strategy, building a culture of engagement, and transforming the workforce into a "winforce." It was the kind of talk that James needed to hear.

With Sarah on board, a sense of cautious optimism began to permeate the executive suite. James knew that the road ahead would be fraught with challenges, but he also believed that with the right leadership, TechSolutions could rise from the ashes.

And so, as Sarah walked into the TechSolutions building on her first day, the stage was set for a transformation that would test the limits of her strategic acumen and the resilience of the entire company. The struggles of the past were clear, but the future held a glimmer of hope. The real work was just beginning.

Introduction of Sarah Thompson as CHRO

It was a crisp Tuesday morning when Sarah Thompson arrived at TechSolutions, ready to step into her new role as Chief Human Resources Officer. As she walked through the glass doors of the building, she was immediately struck by the heavy silence that hung in the air. The once bustling lobby now felt like a ghost town, with employees moving about in a state of quiet resignation.

Sarah adjusted her bag on her shoulder and made her way to the reception desk, where she was greeted by a young, weary-looking receptionist. "Good morning, I'm Sarah Thompson, the new CHRO," she said with a warm smile. The receptionist's eyes lit up with a glimmer of hope, a stark contrast to the atmosphere around her.

CHAPTER 1: THE CATALYST FOR CHANGE

"Welcome, Ms. Thompson. Mr. Parker is expecting you. I'll take you to his office," the receptionist replied, leading Sarah through the maze of cubicles and glass-walled offices.

As they walked, Sarah observed the employees she passed by. Most were hunched over their desks, their faces illuminated by the glow of computer screens. There was little conversation, and even fewer smiles. It was clear to Sarah that the company's struggles were not just financial but deeply cultural.

They arrived at James Parker's office, a corner room with a panoramic view of the city. James stood as they entered, extending a hand to Sarah. "Sarah, it's great to finally have you here. We've been looking forward to your arrival," he said, his tone a mix of relief and anticipation.

"Thank you, James. I'm eager to get started," Sarah replied, shaking his hand firmly. She took a seat across from him, noting the stack of reports and files cluttering his desk.

"I won't sugarcoat it, Sarah. We're in a tough spot. Employee morale is at an all-time low, turnover is through the roof, and our financials are a mess. But I believe you can help us turn things around," James said, his voice heavy with the weight of responsibility.

Sarah nodded, her mind already racing with ideas. "I've reviewed some of the reports and spoken with a few key people. I think we can start by addressing the immediate pain points: talent acquisition, employee engagement, and leadership development. But first, I need to understand the company's DNA. What makes TechSolutions tick?"

James leaned back in his chair, a thoughtful expression on his face. "TechSolutions was built on innovation and collaboration. Our greatest strength was our ability to attract and retain top talent, people who were passionate about what they did and proud to be here. But somewhere along the way, we lost that spark. The rapid growth, the pressures of competition, and a few missteps in leadership have taken their toll."

Sarah listened intently, absorbing every detail. She knew that understanding the past was crucial to shaping the future. "We need to reignite that passion and rebuild the sense of community. It's not just about policies and processes; it's about creating an environment where people feel valued and empowered to do their best work."

James nodded in agreement. "I trust your judgment, Sarah. What do you need from me?"

"Your support and openness to change. We're going to shake things up, and it's going to be uncomfortable at times. But if we're committed to this transformation, we can turn TechSolutions into a place where people are excited to come to work again," Sarah said, her determination evident.

"Consider it done," James replied, a newfound resolve in his voice.

As Sarah left James's office, she felt a mix of excitement and urgency. She had a clear mandate and the CEO's backing. The next step was to meet with the HR team and start laying the groundwork for the changes ahead.

Walking into the HR department, Sarah was greeted by Michelle, the harried HR manager she had heard about. Michelle looked up from her cluttered desk, surprise and curiosity in her eyes. "Sarah Thompson, welcome to TechSolutions," she said, standing up to shake hands.

"Thank you, Michelle. I'm looking forward to working with you. We have a lot to do, and I'm confident we can make a real difference together," Sarah replied, her voice steady and reassuring.

They spent the next few hours discussing the current state of HR, identifying immediate priorities, and outlining the initial steps for the transformation. Sarah's energy and clarity of vision began to infuse a sense of hope and purpose into the team.

By the end of the day, Sarah had a clearer picture of the challenges ahead and a burgeoning plan to tackle them. She knew that turning around TechSolutions would be no small feat, but she was ready. With her strategic acumen and a commitment to restoring the company's innovative spirit, she was determined to lead TechSolutions from a struggling workforce to a dynamic winforce. The journey had just begun.

Initial Assessment of Company Challenges

Sarah Thompson sat in her new office, a space she had already made her own with a few personal touches: a framed photo of her family, a small potted plant, and a stack of HR journals she considered her bibles. She took a deep breath, savoring the calm before the storm. It was time to roll up her sleeves and dive into the heart of TechSolutions' issues.

Her first step was to conduct a comprehensive assessment of the company's current state. Sarah began by poring over data reports and employee surveys. She spent long hours in the office, surrounded by printouts and charts, her keen eyes absorbing the grim statistics. Employee turnover rates were alarmingly high, especially among the most talented staff. The last engagement survey revealed that over 60% of employees felt undervalued and saw no clear career progression.

The numbers were telling, but Sarah knew they were just one piece of the puzzle. She needed to hear the voices behind the data. She scheduled a series of one-on-one interviews with employees across different departments, starting with the senior leadership team.

Her first meeting was with Robert Chen, the Head of Engineering. Robert was a seasoned professional, respected by his peers, but the strain of recent months was evident in the deep lines etched on his face. As they sat down in the conference room, Sarah initiated the conversation with an open-ended question. "Robert, can you tell me about the biggest challenges your team is facing?"

Robert sighed deeply. "Where do I start? We're losing good people faster than we can replace them. The workload keeps increasing, but we don't have enough hands to manage it. It's a vicious cycle—those who stay are overworked and frustrated, which leads to more resignations."

Sarah nodded, making notes. "And what about the new hires? Are they fitting in?"

Robert shook his head. "The onboarding process is practically non-existent. New hires are thrown into the deep end with little support. They either sink or swim, and lately, more are sinking."

Next, Sarah met with Linda Martinez, a mid-level project manager who had been with TechSolutions for over five years. Linda's passion for her work was evident, but so was her frustration. "I used to love this place," she confessed. "But now, it feels like we're just going through the motions. There's no sense of community anymore. We used to have brainstorming sessions, team-building events, even casual Friday lunches. Now, it's all deadlines and deliverables."

"What do you think changed?" Sarah asked, leaning in.

Linda shrugged. "Leadership became more about managing

from above rather than leading from within. There's a disconnect between what the executives want and what's actually happening on the ground. We're not being heard."

Throughout the week, Sarah continued her listening tour, meeting with a diverse cross-section of the workforce. She spoke with young software developers like Cynthia Chen, who expressed her frustration over the lack of mentorship and career development opportunities. "I feel like I'm stagnating," Cynthia said, her voice tinged with disappointment. "I want to grow, to learn new skills, but there's no clear path for that here."

In a candid conversation with the customer support team, she heard about the burnout and high stress levels due to inadequate staffing and overwhelming workloads. "We're the front line," one support agent said, "but it feels like we're the last priority. Customers are angry because we can't give them the support they need, and we're bearing the brunt of it."

The HR department itself was no better off. Michelle, the HR manager, admitted that their systems were outdated, and their processes were reactive rather than proactive. "We're constantly putting out fires," Michelle lamented. "There's no time to think strategically or to implement programs that could actually improve things."

By the end of her assessment, Sarah had a clear and comprehensive understanding of the challenges TechSolutions faced. The issues were deep-rooted and multifaceted: a high turnover rate, lack of effective onboarding, poor communication, insufficient leadership, and a disconnection between the workforce and the executive team. The company's innovative spirit had been buried under layers of frustration and inefficiency.

Sarah compiled her findings into a detailed report, highlighting the most critical areas that needed immediate attention. She was ready to present her assessment to the executive team. But beyond the data and the interviews, Sarah felt a deep sense of empathy and responsibility. The people of TechSolutions were talented and passionate; they just needed the right environment to thrive.

As she prepared her presentation, Sarah's mind was already racing with potential solutions. She envisioned a revitalized TechSolutions where employees were engaged, valued, and empowered. The journey would be challenging, but she was determined to lead the company from a struggling workforce to a dynamic winforce.

The stage was set for change, and Sarah was ready to take the first bold steps.

Executive Team's Expectations and Skepticism

The morning of the executive team meeting dawned gray and rainy, but Sarah Thompson felt a spark of determination as she walked into the TechSolutions headquarters. She had spent days compiling her assessment and was ready to present her findings and vision for the future. As she entered the boardroom, she was greeted by the executive team, their faces a mix of curiosity and skepticism.

James Parker, the CEO, sat at the head of the long conference table, his expression serious but welcoming. "Good morning, everyone. I've asked Sarah to present her initial assessment and recommendations. I believe she has some important insights for us."

Sarah nodded in acknowledgment and began her presentation, her voice steady and confident. She started with the hard facts, laying out the data she had gathered: high turnover rates, low employee engagement, and a disconnect between leadership and the workforce. As she spoke, she watched the faces around the table, noting the varying reactions.

Michael Rivera, the CFO, leaned back in his chair, arms crossed, his expression skeptical. "These numbers are concerning, Sarah, but we've seen them before. What's different this time? What makes you think we can turn this around?"

Sarah met his gaze steadily. "I understand the skepticism, Michael. The difference lies in a strategic, holistic approach to HR. We need to stop treating symptoms and start addressing the root causes. This involves a fundamental shift in how we think about our people and their roles within the company."

She moved on to the qualitative insights, sharing anecdotes and quotes from her conversations with employees. She spoke of Robert Chen's frustrations with the lack of support for new hires, Cynthia Chen's desire for career development, and the burnout plaguing the customer support team. The room grew quieter as the exccutives listened to the human side of the data.

Linda Davis, the Chief Marketing Officer, leaned forward, her brow furrowed. "It's clear that our employees are struggling, but how do we balance this with our business needs? We have aggressive targets to meet, and resources are already stretched thin."

"That's a valid concern," Sarah acknowledged. "But investing in our people is not at odds with our business goals—it's essential to achieving them. A motivated, engaged workforce is more productive and innovative. We need to create an environment where employees feel valued and empowered, which will ultimately drive better business outcomes."

John Avery, the Chief Technology Officer, spoke up next.

"I've seen too many initiatives come and go, Sarah. What makes you think your approach will stick?"

Sarah paused, choosing her words carefully. "Because it's not just about implementing new programs; it's about a cultural transformation. We need to align our HR practices with our strategic goals and make sure that every employee understands their role in our success. This means continuous communication, leadership involvement, and a commitment to long-term change."

She outlined her strategic plan, highlighting key initiatives such as revamping the recruitment process to attract top talent, developing comprehensive onboarding programs, launching leadership development workshops, and implementing continuous feedback mechanisms. As she detailed the steps, she sensed a shift in the room. The initial skepticism was giving way to cautious interest.

James Parker, who had been listening intently, finally spoke. "Thank you, Sarah. It's clear you've put a lot of thought into this. Change is never easy, but it's necessary if we want to regain our competitive edge. I'm fully behind this plan and I expect all of you to support it as well."

Michael Rivera still looked unconvinced. "What about the costs? We're already under financial strain. Can we afford to implement these changes?"

Sarah met his eyes. "We can't afford not to. The cost of inaction is far greater. High turnover, low productivity, and disengaged employees are draining our resources. By investing in strategic HR, we're investing in the future success of TechSolutions. I've prepared a detailed budget, and while there will be upfront costs, the long-term benefits far outweigh them."

CHAPTER 1: THE CATALYST FOR CHANGE

James nodded in agreement. "Michael, we'll review the budget in detail, but I trust Sarah's judgment. We need to think strategically about our investments."

The room fell silent as the executives absorbed the information. Finally, Linda Davis broke the silence. "I'm willing to give this a chance. It's clear we need a new approach."

John Avery nodded. "Agreed. We can't keep doing the same thing and expecting different results."

Michael sighed, his resistance softening. "Alright, let's see how this goes. But we need to monitor progress closely."

Sarah felt a surge of relief and determination. She had won their tentative approval, but the real work was just beginning. "Thank you, everyone. I'm committed to making this transformation a success, and I'll need your support every step of the way."

As the meeting adjourned, James caught Sarah's eye and gave her an encouraging nod. She knew she had a formidable task ahead, but with the executive team's backing, she was ready to lead TechSolutions into a new era of growth and innovation.

The catalyst for change had been set in motion, and Sarah was prepared to navigate the challenges ahead, transforming skepticism into belief and inertia into dynamic action. The journey from workforce to winforce had officially begun.

Sarah's Vision for Strategic HRM

With the executive team's skepticism tempered by cautious optimism, Sarah Thompson seized the opportunity to paint a vivid picture of her vision for Strategic Human Resource Management (HRM) at TechSolutions.

Leaning forward, Sarah met the eyes of each executive in

the room, her voice imbued with passion and conviction. "Strategic HRM isn't just about implementing new programs or policies. It's about fundamentally transforming the way we view and engage with our most valuable asset—our people."

She began by outlining the core principles of strategic HRM: aligning HR initiatives with the company's overarching strategic goals, fostering a culture of continuous learning and development, and empowering employees to reach their full potential. "It's about creating an environment where every member of the team feels valued, heard, and inspired to contribute their best work," she declared.

Sarah emphasized the importance of proactive talent management, highlighting the need to attract and retain top talent, develop robust onboarding processes to set new hires up for success from day one, and implement leadership development programs to cultivate the next generation of TechSolutions leaders.

"We need to shift our focus from reactive problem-solving to proactive planning," Sarah continued. "This means anticipating future workforce needs, identifying skill gaps, and developing targeted strategies to address them. By investing in our employees' growth and development, we not only strengthen our competitive position but also create a more resilient and adaptable organization."

As she spoke, Sarah's vision began to take shape in the minds of the executives. They could see a future where TechSolutions was known not only for its innovative technology but also for its vibrant and engaged workforce—a company that attracted top talent and nurtured a culture of excellence from within.

But Sarah didn't stop there. She outlined a roadmap for implementation, detailing specific initiatives and milestones to track progress along the way. "This won't happen overnight," she cautioned. "But with clear goals, consistent communication, and unwavering commitment from leadership, I believe we can achieve our vision of becoming a true winforce."

The room was silent as Sarah finished her presentation, the weight of her words hanging in the air. James Parker, the CEO, was the first to speak, his voice filled with determination. "Thank you, Sarah. Your vision is bold, but I believe it's exactly what TechSolutions needs. Let's make it happen."

One by one, the other executives voiced their support, their initial skepticism replaced by a newfound sense of purpose. "I'm on board," Linda Davis, the Chief Marketing Officer, declared. "Let's show the industry what TechSolutions is capable of."

Sarah felt a surge of gratitude and determination. The journey ahead would be challenging, but with the executive team aligned behind her vision, she knew that together they could turn TechSolutions into a true winforce—a company where people thrived, innovation flourished, and success was inevitable.

As the meeting adjourned, Sarah glanced out the window at the city skyline, a sense of excitement coursing through her veins. The catalyst for change had been ignited, and she was ready to lead TechSolutions into a new era of growth and prosperity. The journey had begun, and the possibilities were endless.

Setting the Stage for Transformation

With the executive team fully onboard with her vision for Strategic Human Resource Management (HRM), Sarah Thompson wasted no time in laying the groundwork for transformation at TechSolutions.

The first step was to assemble a team of dedicated HR professionals who shared her passion and commitment to change. Sarah handpicked individuals from within the company who had shown potential and a willingness to embrace new ideas. Together, they formed a core team tasked with spearheading the implementation of Sarah's strategic plan.

In a series of intensive brainstorming sessions, the team fleshed out the details of each initiative, outlining specific goals, timelines, and success metrics. They drew inspiration from best practices in HRM, incorporating innovative ideas and cutting-edge technologies to drive efficiency and effectiveness.

But Sarah knew that true transformation went beyond just restructuring processes and systems. It required a shift in mindset—a cultural evolution that would empower employees to take ownership of their roles and contribute to the company's success.

To that end, Sarah launched a company-wide communication campaign, highlighting the importance of the HR transformation and the role that every employee would play in its success. She held town hall meetings, departmental workshops, and one-on-one sessions with team leaders to ensure that everyone understood the vision and felt empowered to contribute.

But perhaps the most pivotal moment came when Sarah unveiled the new mission statement for TechSolutions—a simple yet powerful declaration of purpose that encapsulated the company's commitment to excellence, innovation, and employee empowerment. It became the rallying cry for the entire organization, igniting a sense of pride and unity among employees at all levels.

As the weeks passed, the momentum continued to build. Sarah and her team worked tirelessly to implement the initiatives outlined in the strategic plan, overcoming obstacles and resistance with resilience and determination. They rolled out new recruitment and onboarding processes, launched leadership development programs, and introduced innovative employee engagement initiatives.

And as the changes took root, the impact was palpable. Morale began to improve, turnover rates declined, and productivity soared. Employees felt a renewed sense of purpose and pride in their work, fueled by the knowledge that they were part of something bigger than themselves—a company poised to reclaim its status as a leader in the tech industry.

But Sarah knew that the journey was far from over. The road ahead would be challenging, with obstacles and setbacks inevitable along the way. But she was undeterred, fueled by a vision of a future where TechSolutions was not just a company, but a force for positive change in the world—a true winforce.

And with each small victory, Sarah felt the conviction growing stronger within her. The stage had been set, the players assembled, and the curtain raised on a new chapter in TechSolutions' history. The transformation had begun, and Sarah Thompson was leading the charge, determined to turn her vision into reality.

2

Chapter 2: Charting the Course

Conducting a Comprehensive HR Audit

With the vision for transformation firmly established, Sarah Thompson wasted no time in rolling up her sleeves and diving into the intricate details of TechSolutions' HR landscape. The first order of business: conducting a comprehensive HR audit to assess the strengths, weaknesses, and opportunities for improvement within the organization.

Armed with a meticulous plan and a team of dedicated HR professionals, Sarah embarked on a journey to uncover the hidden gems and untapped potential within TechSolutions' human capital infrastructure.

The audit process was exhaustive, spanning multiple weeks and involving every corner of the company. Sarah and her team poured over mountains of data, scrutinizing everything from employee engagement surveys to performance reviews, from recruitment metrics to training and development programs.

But numbers only told part of the story. Sarah knew that to truly understand the heartbeat of the organization, she needed to hear directly from the people who made it tick. She conducted interviews and focus groups with employees at all levels, from the C-suite to the front lines, listening intently to their hopes, fears, and frustrations.

What emerged was a rich tapestry of insights, illuminating both the triumphs and the tribulations of life at TechSolutions. There were pockets of excellence—teams that had managed to thrive despite the challenges, individuals who embodied the company's values of innovation and collaboration.

But there were also glaring areas of concern—inefficiencies in the recruitment process, disparities in compensation and benefits, and a lack of clear career development pathways. Sarah noted them all, recognizing that each presented an opportunity for improvement and growth.

As the audit drew to a close, Sarah gathered her team to review their findings and distill them into a comprehensive report. They spent long hours poring over the data, analyzing trends, and identifying patterns. And as they did, a clear picture began to emerge—a roadmap for the future of HR at TechSolutions.

But Sarah knew that the real work was just beginning. Armed with the insights gleaned from the audit, she was ready to roll out a series of targeted initiatives aimed at addressing the organization's most pressing HR challenges. The journey ahead would be challenging, but Sarah was undaunted. She had a vision, a plan, and a team of dedicated professionals by her side. And with each step forward, she was one step closer to transforming TechSolutions into the dynamic winforce she knew it could be.

Identifying Key Issues and Bottlenecks

With a sense of urgency, Sarah Thompson delved deep into the heart of TechSolutions, determined to identify the key issues and bottlenecks hindering the company's success. Armed with her strategic mindset and a keen eye for detail, she embarked on a journey of discovery that would shape the course of the company's future.

Sarah began by immersing herself in the daily operations of TechSolutions, shadowing employees in various departments and observing their workflows firsthand. From the bustling development bullpen to the hushed corridors of the HR department, she witnessed the challenges and frustrations faced by employees at every level.

It didn't take long for Sarah to identify the root causes of TechSolutions' struggles. In the development team, she observed a lack of clear direction and communication breakdowns, leading to missed deadlines and subpar quality in deliverables. In the HR department, she discovered outdated processes and systems that were stifling innovation and hampering employee engagement.

But perhaps the most significant bottleneck Sarah uncovered was the disconnect between the executive team and the rest of the organization. Decisions were made in isolation, with little input from those on the front lines who were most affected by them. This lack of transparency and communication had eroded trust and fostered a culture of resentment and disengagement.

Armed with her findings, Sarah wasted no time in presenting her assessment to the executive team. She laid out the key issues and bottlenecks, backing up her observations with data and

CHAPTER 2: CHARTING THE COURSE

real-world examples. The room fell silent as Sarah spoke, her words carrying the weight of truth and urgency.

James Parker, the CEO, listened intently, his brow furrowed with concern. "These are sobering findings, Sarah," he said, his voice grave. "But I'm grateful for your honesty. We can't fix what we don't acknowledge."

The other executives nodded in agreement, their expressions a mix of resignation and determination. They knew that change was long overdue, and Sarah's assessment had laid bare the stark reality of TechSolutions' situation.

But Sarah wasn't content to simply highlight the problems; she was determined to find solutions. Drawing on her years of experience in strategic HRM, she outlined a series of targeted initiatives aimed at addressing the key issues and bottlenecks head-on. From revamping the recruitment process to fostering a culture of open communication and collaboration, Sarah's plan was bold, ambitious, and comprehensive.

As the meeting adjourned, Sarah felt a sense of cautious optimism wash over her. The road ahead would be challenging, but she was ready to lead TechSolutions through the storm. With the support of the executive team and the dedication of the entire organization, she was confident that they could overcome any obstacle and emerge stronger than ever.

The journey of transformation had officially begun, and Sarah Thompson was at the helm, guiding TechSolutions towards a brighter, more prosperous future.

Employee Surveys and Feedback Sessions

With the comprehensive HR audit complete, Sarah Thompson turned her attention to the next crucial step in TechSolutions' transformation journey: gathering feedback directly from the lifeblood of the organization—its employees.

Sarah knew that the key to success lay in understanding the needs, concerns, and aspirations of the people who made TechSolutions tick. And so, armed with surveys, focus groups, and an open-door policy, she embarked on a mission to give every employee a voice in shaping the company's future.

The first phase of the feedback process involved launching a series of company-wide surveys, designed to capture insights on everything from workplace culture to leadership effectiveness. Sarah worked closely with her HR team to craft questions that were both comprehensive and actionable, ensuring that the data collected would provide valuable insights for driving meaningful change.

As the survey responses began to pour in, Sarah and her team huddled together to analyze the data, uncovering trends and patterns that would serve as the foundation for their future initiatives. They were heartened to see a high level of engagement among employees, with many taking the opportunity to share candid feedback and suggestions for improvement.

But Sarah knew that surveys only told part of the story. To truly understand the human side of the data, she organized a series of feedback sessions and focus groups, inviting employees from across the organization to share their experiences and perspectives in a safe and open environment.

The feedback sessions were eye-opening, revealing both

the triumphs and the pain points of life at TechSolutions. Employees spoke passionately about the aspects of their work that they loved—the camaraderie, the sense of purpose, the opportunity to work on cutting-edge projects. But they also didn't shy away from highlighting areas that needed improvement—the lack of transparency in decision-making, the need for better career development opportunities, and the desire for more meaningful recognition and rewards.

Sarah listened intently to every word, taking notes and asking probing questions to ensure that she fully understood the nuances of each employee's experience. She was struck by the passion and dedication of the TechSolutions team, as well as their unwavering commitment to the company's success.

Armed with the insights gathered from the employee surveys and feedback sessions, Sarah and her team set to work developing a series of targeted initiatives aimed at addressing the most pressing concerns raised by employees. From implementing new communication channels to launching mentorship programs and revamping performance management processes, their goal was to create a workplace where every employee felt valued, heard, and empowered to succeed.

As the feedback sessions drew to a close, Sarah felt a sense of gratitude and excitement wash over her. The voices of TechSolutions' employees had spoken, and their input would serve as the guiding light for the company's transformation journey. With their support and collaboration, Sarah was confident that together, they could build a future where TechSolutions thrived as a true winforce in the tech industry.

Analyzing Turnover and Retention Data

As Sarah Thompson delved deeper into TechSolutions' transformation journey, she knew that understanding the company's turnover and retention data was crucial to developing effective strategies for the future. With determination and a keen analytical mind, she set out to uncover the root causes of employee turnover and identify opportunities for improvement.

Sarah began by diving into the wealth of data at her disposal, meticulously analyzing turnover rates, exit interviews, and retention metrics across departments and job roles. What she discovered was both enlightening and concerning—while some turnover was inevitable in any organization, TechSolutions was hemorrhaging talent at an alarming rate, particularly among high-performing employees and those in critical roles.

Armed with this insight, Sarah dug deeper, conducting interviews and focus groups with departing employees to gain a deeper understanding of their reasons for leaving. The stories she heard were varied but often shared common themes—lack of career development opportunities, poor communication from leadership, and a perceived lack of appreciation for their contributions.

But Sarah knew that turnover data alone told only part of the story. To truly understand the impact of employee departures on the organization, she also analyzed retention data, looking at factors such as tenure, performance ratings, and employee engagement levels. What she found was sobering—long-tenured employees were leaving at an alarming rate, and those who remained often reported feeling disengaged and undervalued.

Armed with these insights, Sarah and her team set to work developing targeted strategies aimed at improving employee retention and reducing turnover. They launched initiatives to provide employees with more opportunities for career development and advancement, including training programs, mentorship opportunities, and clear pathways for growth.

They also focused on improving communication and transparency from leadership, ensuring that employees felt informed and included in decision-making processes. Town hall meetings, regular updates from the executive team, and open-door policies were implemented to foster a culture of trust and collaboration.

But perhaps the most impactful initiative was a renewed focus on employee recognition and appreciation. Sarah and her team launched a series of programs aimed at celebrating employee achievements, from monthly awards ceremonies to personalized thank-you notes from leadership. The goal was simple—to show employees that their contributions were valued and appreciated, and to create a workplace where they felt supported and motivated to do their best work.

As the initiatives began to take shape, Sarah monitored progress closely, tracking key metrics and soliciting feedback from employees to ensure that the strategies were having the desired impact. And slowly but surely, she began to see signs of improvement—turnover rates began to decline, and employee engagement levels started to rise.

But Sarah knew that the journey was far from over. Building a culture of retention and engagement was a continuous process, requiring ongoing commitment and dedication from every member of the organization. With determination and a clear vision for the future, Sarah was ready to lead

TechSolutions into a new era of success, one where employees felt valued, supported, and empowered to thrive.

Benchmarking Against Industry Standards

Sarah Thompson understood that for TechSolutions to truly thrive, it needed to not only meet but exceed industry standards in every aspect of its operations, including human resources. With this in mind, she embarked on a journey of benchmarking against industry leaders, determined to identify best practices and areas for improvement.

Armed with mountains of data and a team of dedicated professionals, Sarah dove headfirst into the world of industry benchmarks, scouring reports, studies, and case studies to uncover insights into what made top-performing companies stand out from the rest.

What she found was both enlightening and inspiring. Companies known for their stellar HR practices prioritized employee development, fostered a culture of transparency and trust, and embraced innovation in all aspects of their operations. From cutting-edge recruitment strategies to innovative performance management techniques, these companies set the bar high for excellence in HR.

But Sarah didn't stop at studying industry benchmarks; she also sought out opportunities to learn from the best and brightest in the field. She attended conferences, workshops, and networking events, soaking up knowledge and insights from HR professionals at the forefront of their industry.

Armed with this wealth of information, Sarah and her team set to work identifying areas where TechSolutions could improve and innovate. They developed targeted strategies aimed at aligning the company's HR practices with industry best practices, from revamping recruitment processes to implementing state-of-the-art training and development programs.

But perhaps the most significant impact of benchmarking against industry standards was the shift in mindset it inspired within the organization. Employees at all levels began to see themselves not just as cogs in a machine, but as integral contributors to a company striving for excellence in everything it did.

As the months passed, Sarah monitored progress closely, tracking key metrics and soliciting feedback from employees to ensure that the strategies were having the desired impact. And slowly but surely, she began to see signs of improvement—TechSolutions was becoming known not just for its innovative technology, but for its world-class HR practices as well.

But Sarah knew that the journey was far from over. Building a culture of excellence was a continuous process, requiring ongoing commitment and dedication from every member of the organization. With determination and a clear vision for the future, she was ready to lead TechSolutions into a new era of success—one where excellence was not just a goal, but a way of life.

Presenting Findings to the Leadership Team

After weeks of exhaustive research, Sarah Thompson stood at the precipice of change, armed with insights gleaned from the depths of TechSolutions' operations. With unwavering determination, she prepared to present her findings to the leadership team, knowing that the success of the company's transformation hinged on their buy-in and support.

As she stepped into the boardroom, Sarah's heart pounded with anticipation. The executive team, with James Parker at the helm, sat poised and attentive, ready to hear her assessment of TechSolutions' current state and her vision for the future.

With confidence born of meticulous preparation, Sarah began her presentation, her voice steady and resolute. She laid out the stark realities facing TechSolutions—the high turnover rates, the lack of employee engagement, the disconnect between leadership and the workforce. But she didn't stop there. She also highlighted the opportunities for growth and improvement, the untapped potential waiting to be unleashed.

As she spoke, Sarah could sense the tension in the room, the weight of her words hanging heavy in the air. But she pressed on, backed by data and driven by a vision of a brighter future for TechSolutions.

And then, something remarkable happened. As Sarah outlined her strategic plan for transforming TechSolutions into a true winforce, she saw a spark ignite in the eyes of the executives—a spark of hope, of possibility, of belief in what could be.

James Parker, ever the pragmatist, was the first to speak. "These findings are sobering, Sarah," he said, his voice measured. "But they also represent an opportunity for us to rise to the occasion and chart a new course for TechSolutions."

The other executives nodded in agreement, their expressions a mix of determination and resolve. They could see the potential for greatness within their grasp, and they were ready to seize it with both hands.

But Sarah knew that the journey ahead would not be easy. Transforming TechSolutions would require courage, perseverance, and unwavering commitment from every member of the organization. It would mean challenging the status quo, embracing change, and daring to dream of what could be.

As the meeting adjourned, Sarah felt a sense of pride wash over her. The seeds of change had been planted, and she was honored to be leading the charge. With the support of the leadership team and the dedication of the entire organization, she knew that together, they could turn TechSolutions into a true winforce—a company where innovation thrived, employees flourished, and success was inevitable.

3

Chapter 3: Developing the Strategy

With the foundation laid and the path forward illuminated by Sarah Thompson's vision, TechSolutions stood at the threshold of a new era. Now, the time had come to transform that vision into a concrete strategy—a roadmap for success that would guide the company through the turbulent waters of change.

Sarah convened her core team of HR professionals, their minds buzzing with anticipation and excitement for the task ahead. Together, they huddled in the conference room, surrounded by whiteboards and flip charts, ready to embark on the journey of developing the strategy that would shape TechSolutions' future.

The room hummed with energy as ideas flowed freely, each member of the team bringing their unique perspective and expertise to the table. Sarah listened intently, capturing every suggestion and insight, weaving them together into a tapestry of possibility.

They began by defining the overarching goals of the strategy—building a culture of innovation, fostering employee

CHAPTER 3: DEVELOPING THE STRATEGY

engagement, and driving operational excellence. These goals would serve as the guiding principles for every initiative and decision that followed.

Next, they delved into the specifics, outlining a series of targeted initiatives aimed at achieving each goal. From revamping the recruitment process to implementing new performance management systems, their strategy was bold, ambitious, and comprehensive.

But perhaps the most important aspect of the strategy was its emphasis on people. Sarah and her team recognized that success hinged not just on systems and processes, but on the hearts and minds of the employees who brought them to life. And so, they developed initiatives aimed at empowering employees, fostering a culture of trust and collaboration, and providing opportunities for growth and development at every level.

As the hours stretched into days and the days into weeks, the strategy began to take shape—a living, breathing document that captured the hopes and aspirations of everyone at TechSolutions. It was a roadmap for the future—a vision of what the company could become if they dared to dream big and work tirelessly to make those dreams a reality.

And as Sarah put the finishing touches on the strategy, she felt a sense of pride wash over her. This was more than just a plan—it was a manifesto, a declaration of intent, a call to arms for every member of the TechSolutions family. With this strategy as their guide, there was nothing they couldn't achieve.

The stage was set, the players assembled, and the curtain raised on a new chapter in TechSolutions' history. The journey ahead would be challenging, but with a clear strategy and a team of dedicated professionals by their side, Sarah knew that they were ready to face whatever the future held.

Crafting a Strategic HRM Plan

In the heart of TechSolutions' headquarters, Sarah Thompson and her team of HR professionals gathered around the conference table, ready to embark on the pivotal task of crafting a Strategic Human Resource Management (HRM) plan. With pens poised and minds ablaze with creativity, they delved into the intricate process of mapping out the company's HR future.

Drawing inspiration from industry best practices, cutting-edge research, and the unique culture of TechSolutions, they began by defining the core pillars of the HRM plan—talent acquisition, development, engagement, and retention. These pillars would serve as the guiding principles for every initiative and decision that followed.

With meticulous attention to detail, they outlined a series of targeted initiatives aimed at attracting top talent to TechSolutions, from revamping the recruitment process to building a strong employer brand. They knew that the key to success lay in finding and retaining the best and brightest minds in the industry, and they were determined to leave no stone unturned in their quest.

But talent acquisition was just the beginning. Sarah and her team recognized that the real challenge lay in developing and nurturing that talent once it was through the door. And so, they crafted a comprehensive plan for employee development, including training programs, mentorship opportunities, and leadership development initiatives designed to unlock the full potential of every member of the TechSolutions team.

But perhaps the most crucial aspect of the Strategic HRM

plan was its focus on employee engagement and retention. Sarah knew that in order to succeed, TechSolutions needed a workforce that was not just competent, but passionate and committed to the company's mission and values. And so, they developed initiatives aimed at fostering a culture of trust, transparency, and collaboration, from regular communication channels to recognition and reward programs that celebrated employee achievements.

As the days turned into weeks and the plan took shape, Sarah felt a sense of pride wash over her. This wasn't just a document—it was a blueprint for the future of TechSolutions, a roadmap to success that would guide the company through the challenges and opportunities that lay ahead.

And as she looked around the room at her team, she knew that they were ready for the journey. With their creativity, dedication, and unwavering commitment to excellence, there was no obstacle they couldn't overcome, no goal they couldn't achieve.

The Strategic IIRM plan was complete, and the stage was set for TechSolutions to embark on a new era of growth and prosperity. The future was bright, and Sarah and her team were ready to lead the way.

Aligning HR Initiatives with Business Goals

As the sun rose over the TechSolutions campus, Sarah Thompson and her team gathered once again, their mission clear: to align the company's HR initiatives with its overarching business goals. With determination and purpose, they set out to weave a seamless tapestry of HR strategies that would propel TechSolutions towards success.

At the heart of their endeavor lay a simple yet profound truth: for HR to truly make an impact, it must be tightly integrated with the broader goals and objectives of the organization. And so, armed with this guiding principle, Sarah and her team set to work, analyzing TechSolutions' business strategy with laser focus.

They pored over financial reports, market analyses, and strategic plans, seeking to understand the company's key priorities and challenges. From expanding into new markets to launching innovative products, they left no stone unturned in their quest to uncover the strategic imperatives that would shape TechSolutions' future.

With these insights in hand, they began to craft a series of HR initiatives designed to directly support and enhance the company's business goals. From talent acquisition strategies tailored to meet the needs of emerging markets to employee development programs focused on cultivating the skills required for future innovation, their plan was both bold and pragmatic, ambitious yet achievable.

But perhaps the most important aspect of their approach was its emphasis on partnership and collaboration. Sarah knew that in order to succeed, HR couldn't operate in a vacuum—it needed to work hand-in-hand with every department and function within the organization, from marketing and sales to finance and operations.

And so, they reached out to their colleagues across TechSolutions, seeking input and feedback on how HR could best support their efforts. They listened intently to their concerns and aspirations, incorporating their insights into their planning process and ensuring that their initiatives were truly aligned with the needs of the business.

As the days turned into weeks and their plan took shape, Sarah felt a sense of satisfaction wash over her. This wasn't just HR strategy—it was a blueprint for success, a roadmap that would guide TechSolutions towards its goals and aspirations. And with the support of her team and colleagues across the organization, she knew that they were ready to embark on this journey together, united in their vision of a brighter future for TechSolutions.

Prioritizing Key Areas for Intervention

In the heart of TechSolutions' headquarters, Sarah Thompson and her team huddled together, their brows furrowed with determination as they tackled the daunting task of prioritizing key areas for intervention within the company's HR landscape. With a plethora of challenges and opportunities laid out before them, they knew that their success depended on their ability to focus their efforts where they would have the greatest impact.

Armed with data and insights gathered from exhaustive research and analysis, they began the arduous process of identifying the most pressing issues facing TechSolutions' workforce. They pored over turnover rates, engagement surveys, and performance metrics, searching for patterns and trends that would reveal where intervention was most urgently needed.

As they sifted through the data, a few key areas quickly emerged as top priorities. High turnover rates among key talent pools, stagnant employee engagement levels, and skill gaps in critical areas were among the most glaring issues facing the organization. But rather than feeling overwhelmed, Sarah and her team saw these challenges as opportunities for growth and improvement.

With a clear understanding of where intervention was needed most, they set to work developing targeted strategies aimed at addressing each priority area. They brainstormed innovative solutions, drawing on best practices from within and outside the industry, and carefully weighing the potential impact of each initiative.

But prioritizing key areas for intervention wasn't just about solving immediate problems—it was also about laying the groundwork for long-term success. Sarah and her team knew that in order to truly transform TechSolutions' HR landscape, they needed to take a holistic approach, addressing not just symptoms but root causes.

And so, they developed a comprehensive plan that addressed each priority area in a strategic and systematic way. From launching targeted recruitment campaigns to attract and retain top talent, to implementing employee engagement initiatives designed to foster a culture of trust and collaboration, their plan was bold, ambitious, and forward-thinking.

As the days turned into weeks and their plan took shape, Sarah felt a sense of excitement and anticipation wash over her. This wasn't just about solving problems—it was about laying the foundation for a brighter future for TechSolutions, one where every employee felt valued, engaged, and empowered to do their best work.

With their priorities clear and their plan in place, Sarah and her team were ready to embark on the next phase of their journey. The road ahead would be challenging, but with focus, determination, and a shared commitment to excellence, they knew that they were ready to face whatever challenges lay ahead.

Setting Measurable Objectives and KPIs

In the heart of TechSolutions' headquarters, Sarah Thompson and her team gathered once more, their focus now shifting to the crucial task of setting measurable objectives and Key Performance Indicators (KPIs) that would serve as the yardstick for success in their HR initiatives. With pens poised and minds sharp, they delved into the intricate process of defining clear, quantifiable goals that would guide their efforts and measure their progress.

Drawing on their collective expertise and insights gathered from extensive research and analysis, they began by articulating a set of overarching objectives that aligned with the company's broader goals. From reducing turnover rates to improving employee engagement and driving operational excellence, their objectives were ambitious yet achievable, reflecting their unwavering commitment to excellence in every aspect of HR.

But objectives alone were not enough. In order to track their progress and ensure accountability, they needed to define a set of KPIs that would allow them to measure the success of their initiatives with precision and clarity. And so, they set to work, brainstorming a comprehensive list of metrics that would provide insight into every facet of their HR strategy.

They considered everything from turnover rates and employee satisfaction scores to recruitment metrics and training completion rates, carefully selecting KPIs that would not only reflect the impact of their initiatives but also serve as leading indicators of future success.

But setting KPIs wasn't just about choosing numbers—it was also about ensuring alignment with the company's broader goals and objectives. Sarah and her team took great care to ensure that each KPI was directly linked to a specific objective, creating a clear line of sight from their HR initiatives to the overall success of TechSolutions.

As the hours passed and their list of objectives and KPIs grew longer, Sarah felt a sense of satisfaction wash over her. This wasn't just about setting goals—it was about creating a roadmap for success, a blueprint that would guide their efforts and measure their progress every step of the way.

With their objectives defined and their KPIs in place, Sarah and her team were ready to embark on the next phase of their journey. The road ahead would be challenging, but with clear goals and a solid plan in place, they knew that they were well-equipped to face whatever challenges lay ahead.

Securing Executive Buy-in and Support

In the sleek, high-rise conference room of TechSolutions, Sarah Thompson stood at the head of the table, her gaze steady and determined as she prepared to present the culmination of weeks of hard work: the company's meticulously crafted HR strategy. Around her, the executive team, including CEO James Parker, leaned in with anticipation, their expressions a mix of curiosity and expectation.

With a confident smile, Sarah began to outline the key components of the strategy—the overarching objectives, the targeted initiatives, and the measurable KPIs that would guide their efforts and measure their progress. She spoke passionately, her words infused with the conviction that this plan held the key to TechSolutions' future success.

But as she spoke, she knew that words alone would not be

enough to secure the support of the executive team. They would need to see the vision, feel the urgency, and understand the potential impact of the HR strategy on the company's bottom line.

And so, Sarah backed up her presentation with data—reams of it, meticulously collected and analyzed over weeks of exhaustive research and analysis. She highlighted the sobering realities facing TechSolutions—the high turnover rates, the stagnant employee engagement levels, the skills gaps in critical areas—and made it clear that without intervention, the company's future was at risk.

But she didn't stop there. Sarah also painted a vivid picture of what success could look like with the implementation of their HR strategy—increased employee retention, higher levels of engagement, and a workforce that was not just competent but passionate and committed to the company's mission and values.

As Sarah spoke, she could sense a shift in the room—a growing sense of excitement and possibility, as the executive team began to see the potential of the HR strategy to drive real, tangible results for TechSolutions. They asked probing questions, challenged assumptions, and engaged in lively debate, but beneath it all, there was a sense of shared purpose—a shared belief in the power of HR to transform the company for the better.

And then, as Sarah wrapped up her presentation, she looked around the room at her colleagues, her heart filled with hope and anticipation. The seeds of change had been planted, and she knew that with the support of the executive team, they were ready to embark on this journey together, united in their vision of a brighter future for TechSolutions.

Communicating the Strategy to the Stakeholders

With the executive team firmly on board, Sarah Thompson and her team turned their attention to the next crucial step in their journey: communicating the HR strategy to the wider TechSolutions community. They knew that securing buy-in and support from all stakeholders—from frontline employees to middle managers—was essential for the success of their initiatives.

And so, armed with a clear vision and a compelling narrative, they set out to spread the word, engaging stakeholders at every level of the organization through a series of targeted communication efforts.

They began by crafting a comprehensive communication plan, outlining key messages, channels, and timelines for sharing the HR strategy with the TechSolutions community. From town hall meetings and departmental briefings to email updates and intranet posts, they left no stone unturned in their quest to ensure that every employee had a clear understanding of the company's vision and goals.

But communicating the strategy wasn't just about sharing information—it was also about inspiring and engaging employees, rallying them behind a shared vision of success. And so, Sarah and her team worked tirelessly to craft messaging that resonated with TechSolutions' diverse workforce, highlighting the impact of the HR strategy on their day-to-day lives and the opportunities it presented for growth and development.

They enlisted the help of champions and advocates from within the organization—employees who were passionate about the company's mission and eager to share their enthusiasm with their colleagues. These champions served as

CHAPTER 3: DEVELOPING THE STRATEGY

ambassadors for the HR strategy, spreading the word and building excitement among their peers.

As the days turned into weeks and their communication efforts gained momentum, Sarah could sense a shift in the culture at TechSolutions. Employees were engaged, energized, and eager to play their part in bringing the company's vision to life. From water cooler conversations to virtual brainstorming sessions, the buzz of excitement was palpable, as people across the organization came together to shape the future of TechSolutions.

And as Sarah looked around at the faces of her colleagues, she knew that their efforts had paid off. The HR strategy wasn't just a document—it was a living, breathing testament to the power of communication and collaboration, a blueprint for success that had been embraced by every member of the TechSolutions family.

With their stakeholders firmly on board, Sarah and her team were ready to take the next step in their journey, confident in their ability to turn their vision into reality and lead TechSolutions to new heights of success.

4

Chapter 4: Talent Acquisition and Recruitment

In the bustling heart of the TechSolutions headquarters, the air was charged with anticipation as Sarah Thompson and her team prepared to embark on the crucial task of talent acquisition and recruitment. With the company's ambitious HR strategy as their guide, they set out to attract and onboard the best and brightest minds in the industry, fueling the company's growth and innovation.

Armed with a deep understanding of TechSolutions' culture, values, and strategic objectives, they began by crafting a compelling employer brand—one that would resonate with top talent and set TechSolutions apart as an employer of choice. From sleek recruitment materials to engaging social media campaigns, they worked tirelessly to showcase the company's unique culture and exciting opportunities for growth.

But talent acquisition was more than just marketing—it was about finding the right people for the right roles. And so, they developed a targeted recruitment strategy, leveraging a mix of traditional and innovative approaches to identify and attract top talent from across the globe. From job fairs and networking events to targeted LinkedIn campaigns and employee referrals, they left no stone unturned in their quest to find the perfect fit for every position.

As the resumes poured in and the interviews began, Sarah and her team approached each candidate with care and diligence, seeking not just technical skills but also cultural fit and alignment with TechSolutions' values. They asked probing questions, listened intently to each candidate's story, and evaluated their potential to contribute to the company's success.

But talent acquisition didn't end with making the hire—it was also about setting new employees up for success from day one. And so, they developed a comprehensive onboarding program, designed to immerse new hires in the company's culture, values, and ways of working. From orientation sessions and buddy programs to personalized training plans, they ensured that every new employee felt welcomed, supported, and empowered to make a difference from the very beginning.

As the weeks turned into months and the talent acquisition and recruitment efforts bore fruit, Sarah felt a sense of pride wash over her. This wasn't just about filling seats—it was about building a team of passionate, talented individuals who shared a common vision and commitment to excellence. And with every new hire that walked through the doors of TechSolutions, she knew that they were one step closer to realizing their vision of success.

Redesigning the Recruitment Process

In the heart of TechSolutions' bustling HR department, Sarah Thompson and her team gathered for a pivotal meeting—the kickoff of their mission to redesign the company's recruitment process. With the goal of attracting top talent and fostering a culture of innovation, they knew that reimagining their approach to recruitment was essential to their success.

As they brainstormed ideas and strategies, a sense of excitement filled the room. This wasn't just about making small tweaks—it was about completely overhauling the way TechSolutions attracted and onboarded new talent, creating a process that was efficient, effective, and aligned with the company's strategic objectives.

With creativity and determination, they began by identifying pain points and bottlenecks in the existing recruitment process, from cumbersome paperwork to lengthy hiring timelines. Armed with this insight, they set to work developing a streamlined, candidate-centric approach that would delight applicants and hiring managers alike.

They embraced technology, implementing cutting-edge applicant tracking systems and video interviewing platforms to streamline the hiring process and improve the candidate experience. They also revamped job descriptions and career pages, infusing them with personality and authenticity to attract top talent and showcase TechSolutions' unique culture and values.

But perhaps the most important aspect of the redesigned recruitment process was its focus on diversity and inclusion. Sarah and her team recognized that building a truly innovative and high-performing team required a diverse range of perspectives and experiences, and so they developed initiatives to attract and retain talent from underrepresented groups.

From targeted outreach to diverse candidates to unconscious bias training for hiring managers, they worked tirelessly to create an inclusive environment where every individual felt valued, respected, and empowered to succeed.

As the weeks passed and the redesigned recruitment process took shape, Sarah felt a sense of pride wash over her. This wasn't just about filling open positions—it was about building a team that reflected the rich tapestry of humanity, a team that was stronger and more resilient because of its diversity.

With the redesigned recruitment process in place, Sarah and her team were ready to take the next step in their journey, confident that they were well-equipped to attract and onboard the best and brightest talent in the industry. And as they looked ahead to the future, they knew that the possibilities were endless.

Developing Employer Branding Strategies

In the vibrant heart of TechSolutions' marketing department, Sarah Thompson and her team gathered to embark on a mission critical to the company's success: developing employer branding strategies that would attract top talent and position TechSolutions as an employer of choice in the competitive market.

With a fervent dedication to showcasing the company's unique culture, values, and opportunities, they delved into the task with passion and creativity. They knew that in order to stand out in a crowded field, they needed to craft a compelling narrative—one that would resonate with prospective candidates and set TechSolutions apart from the competition.

Drawing inspiration from the company's rich history, innovative spirit, and commitment to excellence, they set to work developing a series of employer branding initiatives that would capture the imagination of job seekers and showcase the unique opportunities available at TechSolutions.

They started by revamping the company's career website, infusing it with vibrant visuals, engaging content, and authentic employee stories that brought the company's culture and values to life. From behind-the-scenes videos to employee testimonials, they left no stone unturned in their quest to paint a vivid picture of what it was like to work at TechSolutions.

But they didn't stop there. They also launched targeted employer branding campaigns across a variety of channels, from social media platforms to industry events and job fairs. They leveraged the power of storytelling to highlight TechSolutions' commitment to diversity and inclusion, innovation, and employee development, capturing the attention of top talent and inspiring them to join the TechSolutions family.

As the campaigns gained momentum and the company's employer brand began to take shape, Sarah felt a sense of pride wash over her. This wasn't just about attracting candidates—it was about building a community, a tribe of passionate individuals who shared a common vision and commitment to excellence.

With their employer branding strategies in place, Sarah and her team were ready to take the next step in their journey, confident that they were well-equipped to attract top talent and build a team that would drive TechSolutions forward into a future filled with endless possibilities.

Implementing a Talent Management System

In the nerve center of TechSolutions' HR department, Sarah Thompson and her team convened for a pivotal meeting—the launch of their mission to implement a state-of-the-art Talent Management System (TMS). With the goal of revolutionizing how the company identified, nurtured, and developed talent, they knew that this initiative would be a game-changer for TechSolutions.

With a sense of purpose and determination, they began by assessing the company's current talent management processes, identifying inefficiencies and areas for improvement. Armed with this knowledge, they set out to find a TMS that would streamline their workflows, enhance collaboration, and empower employees to reach their full potential.

After careful consideration, they selected a cutting-edge TMS that offered a suite of tools and features designed to meet TechSolutions' unique needs. From robust performance management modules to advanced analytics and reporting capabilities, it was a solution that promised to revolutionize the way the company managed its talent.

But implementing a TMS wasn't just about installing software—it was about fundamentally transforming how the company approached talent management. And so, Sarah and her team embarked on a comprehensive change management process, engaging stakeholders across the organization and providing training and support to ensure a smooth transition.

They worked closely with department heads and team leaders to define clear goals and expectations for the TMS, aligning its implementation with TechSolutions' broader strategic objectives. They also developed customized training programs to empower employees to make the most of the new system, ensuring that everyone was equipped with the skills and knowledge they needed to succeed.

As the TMS went live and employees began to familiarize themselves with its features and capabilities, Sarah felt a sense of excitement and anticipation wash over her. This wasn't just about upgrading software—it was about empowering employees, unlocking their full potential, and driving TechSolutions forward into a future filled with endless possibilities.

With the TMS in place, Sarah and her team were ready to take the next step in their journey, confident that they were well-equipped to attract, develop, and retain top talent and build a team that would propel TechSolutions to new heights of success.

Building Strategic Partnerships with Universities

In the heart of TechSolutions' corporate headquarters, Sarah Thompson and her team gathered with a sense of purpose and determination. Their mission: to forge strategic partnerships with universities—a key pillar in their talent acquisition and recruitment strategy.

With the goal of tapping into the fresh talent pool of the next generation, they embarked on a journey to establish relationships with top universities renowned for their programs in engineering, computer science, and business. They saw these partnerships not only as a means of attracting top talent but also as an opportunity to shape curricula, provide real-world experience, and foster a pipeline of future leaders for TechSolutions.

Armed with a compelling value proposition, they reached

out to university deans, professors, and career services departments, eager to explore opportunities for collaboration. They spoke passionately about TechSolutions' commitment to innovation, its dynamic work culture, and its exciting opportunities for career growth and development.

But building strategic partnerships wasn't just about signing agreements—it was about forging meaningful relationships built on trust, mutual respect, and shared values. And so, Sarah and her team invested time and effort in getting to know their university partners, listening to their needs and aspirations, and finding common ground.

Together, they brainstormed innovative ways to collaborate, from internship programs and co-op placements to joint research projects and guest lectures. They also offered mentorship and networking opportunities for students, providing them with valuable insights into the world of work and helping them develop the skills and confidence they needed to succeed.

As the partnerships took root and flourished, Sarah felt a sense of pride wash over her. This wasn't just about recruiting talent—it was about investing in the next generation, nurturing their potential, and shaping the future of the industry.

With strategic partnerships with universities in place, Sarah and her team were ready to take the next step in their journey, confident that they were well-equipped to attract top talent and build a team that would drive TechSolutions forward into a future filled with endless possibilities.

Enhancing the Candidate Experience

In the heart of TechSolutions' HR department, Sarah Thompson and her team convened for a crucial discussion—how to enhance the candidate experience and leave a lasting impression on every individual who crossed the company's threshold. They understood that in today's competitive job market, the candidate experience was more than just a formality—it was a reflection of TechSolutions' culture, values, and commitment to excellence.

With a shared commitment to creating memorable experiences for candidates, they set out to reimagine every touchpoint of the recruitment process, from initial contact to final offer. They wanted candidates to feel valued, respected, and excited about the possibility of joining the TechSolutions family.

They started by revamping the company's careers website, ensuring that it was user-friendly, informative, and visually appealing. They also streamlined the application process, making it easy for candidates to submit their materials and track their progress every step of the way.

But enhancing the candidate experience wasn't just about technology—it was also about human connection. And so, Sarah and her team took great care to personalize their interactions with candidates, responding promptly to inquiries, providing regular updates on the status of their applications, and offering support and guidance throughout the recruitment process.

They also made sure to create a warm and welcoming environment for candidates during interviews and assessments, ensuring that they felt comfortable and at ease as they showcased their skills and experience. From greeting them with a smile to providing refreshments and a tour of the office, every detail was carefully considered to leave a positive impression.

As the recruitment process unfolded and candidates began to share their experiences with friends and colleagues, Sarah felt a sense of satisfaction wash over her. This wasn't just about filling open positions—it was about building relationships, nurturing connections, and leaving a lasting impact on every individual who crossed their path.

With the candidate experience enhanced and the recruitment process optimized, Sarah and her team were ready to take the next step in their journey, confident that they were well-equipped to attract and retain top talent and build a team that would drive TechSolutions forward into a future filled with endless possibilities.

Metrics for Recruitment Success

In the heart of TechSolutions' HR department, Sarah Thompson and her team gathered around a conference table, their eyes fixed on the screen displaying a dashboard of recruitment metrics. With a sense of purpose and determination, they delved into the task of measuring the success of their recruitment efforts—a crucial step in their quest to attract and retain top talent.

Armed with data and insights gathered from the company's applicant tracking system, they began by analyzing key metrics that would provide insight into the effectiveness of their recruitment strategies. From the number of applications received to the quality of candidates sourced, they left no stone unturned in their quest to understand what was working—and what wasn't.

They also looked at metrics related to diversity and inclusion, tracking the representation of underrepresented groups in the candidate pool and evaluating the impact of their initiatives to attract and retain diverse talent. They knew that building a truly innovative and high-performing team required a diverse range of perspectives and experiences, and so they made it a priority to measure their progress in this area.

But metrics for recruitment success weren't just about quantity—they were also about quality. And so, Sarah and her team developed a set of benchmarks and standards to evaluate the caliber of candidates being hired, from technical skills and experience to cultural fit and alignment with TechSolutions' values.

As they pored over the data and discussed their findings, Sarah felt a sense of satisfaction wash over her. This wasn't just about crunching numbers—it was about gaining insights that would inform their future recruitment efforts, enabling them to continuously improve and refine their strategies.

With their metrics for recruitment success in hand, Sarah and her team were ready to take the next step in their journey, confident that they were well-equipped to attract and retain top talent and build a team that would drive TechSolutions forward into a future filled with endless possibilities.

5

Chapter 5: Onboarding and Integration

In the bustling corridors of TechSolutions, a new chapter in the company's journey was about to unfold. Sarah Thompson and her team gathered with a sense of purpose and excitement as they prepared to dive into the critical task of onboarding and integration—a pivotal stage in their quest to build a high-performing team.

With a steadfast commitment to ensuring that every new hire felt welcomed, supported, and empowered from day one, they set out to design an onboarding experience that would set the stage for success. They understood that onboarding wasn't just about paperwork and protocols—it was about building connections, fostering a sense of belonging, and equipping employees with the tools and resources they needed to thrive.

Armed with this guiding principle, they set to work crafting a comprehensive onboarding program that reflected TechSolutions' unique culture, values, and ways of working. From orientation sessions and welcome events to personalized training plans and mentorship opportunities, they left no stone unturned in their quest to create a memorable and impactful onboarding experience.

But onboarding wasn't just a one-time event—it was an ongoing process that extended far beyond the first day on the job. And so, Sarah and her team developed a series of touchpoints and check-ins to support new hires as they navigated their first weeks and months at TechSolutions. They provided regular feedback and guidance, answered questions and addressed concerns, and celebrated milestones and achievements along the way.

As the onboarding program unfolded and new hires began to settle into their roles, Sarah felt a sense of pride wash over her. This wasn't just about integrating individuals into the company—it was about weaving them into the fabric of the TechSolutions family, where they would contribute their unique talents and perspectives to the company's collective success.

With the onboarding and integration process underway, Sarah and her team were ready to take the next step in their journey, confident that they were well-equipped to build a team that would drive TechSolutions forward into a future filled with endless possibilities.

Creating a Comprehensive Onboarding Program

In the heart of TechSolutions' vibrant office space, Sarah Thompson and her team gathered around a conference table, their laptops open and pens poised as they embarked on a mission critical to the company's success: creating a comprehensive onboarding program that would set new hires up for success from day one.

CHAPTER 5: ONBOARDING AND INTEGRATION

With a keen understanding of the importance of a well-designed onboarding experience, they set out to craft a program that would not only introduce new hires to the ins and outs of TechSolutions but also foster a sense of belonging and purpose within the organization.

They began by mapping out the onboarding journey from start to finish, identifying key touchpoints and milestones along the way. From the moment a new hire received their offer letter to their first day on the job and beyond, every step was carefully planned and executed to ensure a seamless and memorable experience.

The program kicked off with a warm welcome from Sarah herself, who personally greeted each new hire and shared her excitement about having them join the TechSolutions family. From there, new employees were guided through a series of orientation sessions and onboarding activities designed to familiarize them with the company's culture, values, and ways of working.

But the onboarding program wasn't just about information—it was also about connection. Sarah and her team organized networking events and team-building activities to help new hires forge connections with their colleagues and build relationships that would support them in their roles.

They also provided personalized training and development opportunities tailored to each new hire's role and level of experience, ensuring that they had the skills and knowledge they needed to hit the ground running.

As the onboarding program took shape and new hires began to experience its benefits firsthand, Sarah felt a sense of satisfaction wash over her. This wasn't just about checking boxes—it was about creating a welcoming and supportive environment where every employee felt valued, respected, and empowered to do their best work.

With the comprehensive onboarding program in place, Sarah and her team were ready to take the next step in their journey, confident that they were well-equipped to build a team that would drive TechSolutions forward into a future filled with endless possibilities.

Engaging New Hires from Day One

In the heart of TechSolutions' bustling office, Sarah Thompson and her team gathered with a sense of purpose and excitement as they prepared to tackle the next phase of their onboarding and integration efforts: engaging new hires from day one.

Understanding that the first few days at a new job can be both exhilarating and overwhelming, they were determined to create a welcoming and inclusive environment where every new hire felt valued, supported, and excited about their role at TechSolutions.

With this goal in mind, they set out to design a series of activities and initiatives aimed at immersing new hires in the company's culture, values, and ways of working from the moment they walked through the door.

The day began with a warm welcome from Sarah and the rest of the leadership team, who greeted each new hire with a smile and a handshake, making them feel instantly at ease. They then led the group on a tour of the office, introducing them to their colleagues and showing them the various amenities and resources available to them.

But the engagement didn't stop there. Throughout the day, new hires were invited to participate in a series of interactive sessions and team-building activities designed to foster connections and build camaraderie. From icebreaker games and group exercises to lunchtime meet-and-greets with senior leaders, every moment was carefully curated to ensure that new hires felt included and valued.

In addition to these group activities, Sarah and her team also made sure to provide individualized attention and support to each new hire, answering questions, addressing concerns, and offering guidance as needed. They wanted every employee to feel like they had a support system in place from day one—a network of colleagues who were invested in their success and eager to help them thrive.

As the day drew to a close and new hires began to settle into their roles, Sarah couldn't help but feel a sense of satisfaction wash over her. This wasn't just about onboarding—it was about building a community, a team of passionate individuals who shared a common vision and commitment to excellence.

With new hires engaged and excited about their future at TechSolutions, Sarah and her team were ready to take the next step in their journey, confident that they were well-equipped to build a team that would drive the company forward into a future filled with endless possibilities.

Role-Specific Training and Development Plans

In the heart of TechSolutions' training center, Sarah Thompson and her team gathered around a whiteboard, their faces illuminated by the glow of the projector as they delved into the next phase of their onboarding and integration efforts: crafting role-specific training and development plans for new hires.

Understanding that every role at TechSolutions required

unique skills and knowledge, they were determined to provide new hires with the tools and resources they needed to excel in their positions from day one.

With this goal in mind, they began by conducting a thorough analysis of each new hire's role, identifying the key competencies and areas for development. From technical skills to industry knowledge and soft skills, they left no stone unturned in their quest to create tailored training plans that would set new hires up for success.

Armed with this information, they set to work developing a series of training modules and workshops designed to address the specific needs of each role. From coding boot camps and product deep dives to customer service simulations and leadership seminars, every aspect of the training program was carefully curated to ensure relevance and effectiveness.

But role-specific training wasn't just about imparting knowledge—it was also about providing new hires with opportunities for growth and development. And so, Sarah and her team incorporated elements of mentorship and coaching into the training program, pairing new hires with experienced employees who could provide guidance and support as they navigated their roles.

As the training program unfolded and new hires began to immerse themselves in their role-specific training, Sarah couldn't help but feel a sense of pride wash over her. This wasn't just about onboarding—it was about investing in the future of TechSolutions, nurturing the talents of its employees, and empowering them to reach their full potential.

With role-specific training and development plans in place, Sarah and her team were ready to take the next step in their journey, confident that they were well-equipped to build a team that would drive TechSolutions forward into a future filled with endless possibilities.

Mentorship and Buddy Systems

In the vibrant corridors of TechSolutions, Sarah Thompson and her team gathered to discuss the implementation of mentorship and buddy systems—a crucial aspect of their onboarding and integration efforts. Recognizing the importance of providing new hires with guidance and support as they acclimated to their roles, they were determined to pair each newcomer with a mentor or buddy who could help them navigate their journey at TechSolutions.

With this goal in mind, they set out to identify individuals within the company who exemplified TechSolutions' values and possessed the expertise and experience to serve as effective mentors and buddies.

Drawing from a diverse pool of talent across departments and levels, they carefully matched each new hire with a mentor or buddy who shared their interests, goals, and aspirations. They wanted to create meaningful connections that went beyond the professional realm—connections built on trust, mutual respect, and a shared commitment to growth and development.

As the mentorship and buddy systems were put into place, Sarah and her team watched with satisfaction as new hires and their mentors or buddies forged connections and built relationships that would support them in their roles.

From shadowing sessions and one-on-one meetings to informal coffee chats and lunchtime walks, mentors and buddies provided new hires with valuable insights, advice, and encouragement as they navigated the complexities of their new environment.

But mentorship and buddy systems weren't just about providing support—they were also about fostering a sense of belonging and community within the organization. By pairing new hires with seasoned employees who could offer guidance and perspective, Sarah and her team were creating a culture of collaboration and camaraderie—a culture where everyone felt valued, respected, and empowered to succeed.

With the mentorship and buddy systems in place, Sarah and her team were ready to take the next step in their journey, confident that they were well-equipped to build a team that would drive TechSolutions forward into a future filled with endless possibilities.

Measuring Onboarding Effectiveness

In the heart of TechSolutions' analytics department, Sarah Thompson and her team gathered around a series of monitors displaying graphs and charts, their expressions focused and determined. They had reached a crucial juncture in their onboarding and integration efforts: measuring the effectiveness of their initiatives.

Understanding the importance of evaluating their onboarding process to ensure its success, they delved into the task with precision and purpose.

Armed with data collected from surveys, feedback forms, and performance metrics, they began to analyze the impact of their onboarding efforts on new hires' satisfaction, engagement, and performance.

They looked at indicators such as time to productivity,

retention rates, and employee satisfaction scores, using them as benchmarks to gauge the effectiveness of their onboarding program.

As they pored over the data, patterns began to emerge. They saw that new hires who had participated in mentorship programs and buddy systems reported higher levels of satisfaction and engagement. They also found that those who had received role-specific training and development were quicker to reach full productivity in their roles.

But measuring onboarding effectiveness wasn't just about crunching numbers—it was also about gathering qualitative feedback from new hires and their managers, capturing their experiences and insights to inform future improvements.

And so, Sarah and her team conducted interviews and focus groups, soliciting input from stakeholders across the organization to gain a comprehensive understanding of the onboarding process.

As they analyzed the data and discussed their findings, Sarah felt a sense of satisfaction wash over her. This wasn't just about evaluating their efforts—it was about continuously striving for excellence, refining their processes, and ensuring that every new hire had the best possible experience at TechSolutions.

With their onboarding effectiveness measured and validated, Sarah and her team were ready to take the next step in their journey, confident that they were well-equipped to build a team that would drive TechSolutions forward into a future filled with endless possibilities.

Continuous Improvement in Onboarding Processes

In the heart of TechSolutions' innovation hub, Sarah Thompson and her team convened for a critical discussion on the final subpoint of their onboarding and integration efforts: continuous improvement in onboarding processes. Understanding that excellence was not a destination but a journey, they were determined to evolve and refine their onboarding program to ensure it remained effective and impactful.

With a commitment to innovation and agility, they set out to identify areas for improvement, leveraging data and feedback gathered from new hires, mentors, managers, and other stakeholders.

Armed with this valuable insight, they brainstormed ideas and strategies to enhance the onboarding experience, seeking to streamline processes, address pain points, and introduce new initiatives that would further support new hires as they acclimated to their roles.

They explored the possibility of incorporating gamification elements into the onboarding process, transforming mundane tasks into engaging challenges that would motivate and inspire new hires.

They also considered expanding the mentorship and buddy systems to include cross-functional pairings, allowing new hires to gain exposure to different areas of the company and expand their networks.

But continuous improvement wasn't just about adding new features—it was also about refining existing ones. Sarah and her team conducted thorough evaluations of each component of the onboarding program, looking for opportunities to optimize and enhance the experience for new hires.

CHAPTER 5: ONBOARDING AND INTEGRATION

They fine-tuned training modules, updated orientation materials, and redesigned onboarding checklists to ensure they remained relevant and effective in meeting the evolving needs of the organization.

As they discussed their plans for continuous improvement, Sarah felt a sense of excitement and optimism wash over her. This wasn't just about making incremental changes—it was about fostering a culture of innovation and excellence, where every member of the TechSolutions team was empowered to contribute their ideas and drive positive change.

With their commitment to continuous improvement reaffirmed, Sarah and her team were ready to embark on the next phase of their journey, confident that they were well-equipped to build a team that would drive TechSolutions forward into a future filled with endless possibilities.

6

Chapter 6: Employee Engagement and Retention

In the heart of TechSolutions' bustling headquarters, Sarah Thompson and her team gathered with a sense of purpose and determination as they embarked on the next chapter of their journey: employee engagement and retention. Understanding that the success of the company depended on the commitment and satisfaction of its employees, they were determined to create a workplace where every individual felt valued, respected, and empowered to thrive.

With this goal in mind, they set out to explore the factors that contributed to employee engagement and retention, seeking to understand what motivated employees to go above and beyond in their roles and what kept them committed to the company for the long term.

Armed with insights gathered from surveys, focus groups, and one-on-one interviews, they delved into the task with enthusiasm, eager to uncover the keys to building a culture of engagement and retention at TechSolutions.

They found that factors such as opportunities for growth

and development, meaningful work, and a supportive work environment were crucial in driving employee engagement and retention. Employees wanted to feel challenged, appreciated, and connected to the company's mission and values—they wanted to know that their contributions mattered and that their voices were heard.

With this understanding, Sarah and her team set to work developing a series of initiatives and programs aimed at fostering employee engagement and retention. From mentorship and coaching programs to recognition and rewards initiatives, they left no stone unturned in their quest to create a workplace where every employee felt valued and supported.

But employee engagement and retention weren't just about perks and programs—it was also about fostering a sense of belonging and community within the organization. Sarah and her team organized team-building activities, social events, and community service projects to help employees forge connections with their colleagues and build relationships that would support them in their roles.

As the initiatives and programs took shape and employees began to reap the benefits, Sarah couldn't help but feel a sense of pride wash over her. This wasn't just about retention rates and engagement scores—it was about creating a workplace where every individual felt empowered to bring their whole selves to work, where they could grow, thrive, and make a difference.

With their focus on employee engagement and retention unwavering, Sarah and her team were ready to take the next step in their journey, confident that they were well-equipped to build a team that would drive TechSolutions forward into a future filled with endless possibilities.

Understanding Drivers of Employee Engagement

In the heart of TechSolutions' conference room, Sarah Thompson and her team gathered around a table strewn with papers and charts, their faces illuminated by the glow of the projector. They were on a mission: to unravel the intricacies of employee engagement and uncover the factors that drove TechSolutions' workforce to excel.

With a commitment to understanding the heartbeat of their organization, they delved into surveys, feedback forms, and one-on-one interviews, seeking to gain insight into what motivated employees to bring their best selves to work each day.

As they sifted through the data, patterns began to emerge. They found that employees were most engaged when they felt a sense of purpose and meaning in their work—when they understood how their contributions fit into the larger mission of the company and how they could make a difference.

They also discovered that opportunities for growth and development played a critical role in driving employee engagement. Employees wanted to know that their organization was invested in their professional development—that there were opportunities for advancement, skill-building, and learning.

But perhaps most importantly, they found that relationships were at the heart of employee engagement. Employees valued the connections they forged with their colleagues and managers—they wanted to feel supported, respected, and valued for who they were.

With these insights in hand, Sarah and her team set to work developing strategies to enhance employee engagement at TechSolutions. They created opportunities for employees to connect with one another, both in and out of the office. They launched mentorship programs, coaching initiatives, and peer support networks, fostering a culture of collaboration and camaraderie.

As they reflected on their findings, Sarah couldn't help but feel a sense of excitement. This wasn't just about improving engagement scores—it was about creating a workplace where every employee felt valued, supported, and empowered to do their best work.

With their understanding of the drivers of employee engagement deepened, Sarah and her team were ready to take the next step in their journey, confident that they were well-equipped to build a team that would drive TechSolutions forward into a future filled with endless possibilities.

Developing an Engagement Strategy

In the vibrant meeting room of TechSolutions, Sarah Thompson and her team gathered around a whiteboard, markers in hand, ready to craft the blueprint for their engagement strategy. With a clear understanding of the drivers of employee engagement, they were determined to translate their insights into action—a plan that would ignite passion and commitment among TechSolutions' workforce.

With creativity and enthusiasm, they began to brainstorm ideas, drawing from best practices and innovative approaches to engagement from across industries. They knew that a one-size-fits-all approach wouldn't suffice—that their strategy needed to be tailored to the unique culture and needs of TechSolutions.

They started by identifying key areas where they could make

the most impact. From fostering a culture of recognition and appreciation to providing opportunities for growth and development, they left no stone unturned in their quest to create an environment where every employee felt valued and empowered to succeed.

They also considered the importance of communication and transparency, recognizing that employees wanted to feel informed and involved in the decision-making process. They developed strategies to keep employees updated on company news and initiatives, soliciting feedback and ideas to ensure that their voices were heard.

But perhaps most importantly, they recognized the power of leadership in driving employee engagement. They worked closely with senior leaders to align their actions and behaviors with the company's values, modeling the kind of engagement and commitment they hoped to inspire in others.

As the engagement strategy took shape, Sarah felt a sense of pride wash over her. This wasn't just about implementing a series of initiatives—it was about fostering a cultural shift, a transformation in how employees thought, felt, and acted within the organization.

With their engagement strategy finalized, Sarah and her team were ready to take the next step in their journey, confident that they were well-equipped to build a team that would drive TechSolutions forward into a future filled with endless possibilities.

Implementing Recognition and Reward Programs

In the heart of TechSolutions' headquarters, Sarah Thompson and her team gathered around a table adorned with colorful charts and graphs, their faces illuminated by the glow of the projector. They were on a mission—to implement recognition and reward programs that would celebrate the contributions of TechSolutions' workforce and foster a culture of appreciation and excellence.

With a commitment to recognizing the hard work and dedication of their employees, they set to work developing a range of initiatives designed to acknowledge and reward outstanding performance.

They started by creating a system of peer-to-peer recognition, allowing employees to nominate their colleagues for their contributions and achievements. Whether it was going above and beyond on a project or embodying the company's values in their day-to-day work, every act of excellence was celebrated and acknowledged.

But recognition wasn't just about awards and accolades—it was also about creating opportunities for growth and development. Sarah and her team developed a program that rewarded employees with opportunities for career advancement, skill-building, and learning. Whether it was attending conferences, participating in training programs, or taking on new challenges, employees were given the chance to pursue their passions and expand their horizons.

They also considered the importance of celebrating milestones and achievements, both big and small. From work anniversaries to project milestones, every accomplishment was met with applause and appreciation, reinforcing the sense of pride and camaraderie within the organization.

As the recognition and reward programs were put into place, Sarah couldn't help but feel a sense of excitement and optimism. This wasn't just about boosting morale and motivation—it was about building a culture where every employee felt valued, respected, and empowered to reach their full potential.

With their commitment to recognition and reward solidified, Sarah and her team were ready to take the next step in their journey, confident that they were well-equipped to build a team that would drive TechSolutions forward into a future filled with endless possibilities.

Conducting Regular Employee Surveys

In the heart of TechSolutions' bustling headquarters, Sarah Thompson and her team gathered around a conference table, laptops open and pens poised as they prepared to embark on a critical mission: conducting regular employee surveys.

Understanding that feedback was the lifeblood of any successful organization, they were determined to gather insights from TechSolutions' workforce to inform their engagement and retention efforts.

With this goal in mind, they crafted a comprehensive survey designed to gauge employee satisfaction, identify areas for improvement, and uncover opportunities to enhance the employee experience.

They asked employees about their perceptions of company culture, their level of job satisfaction, and their feelings about opportunities for growth and development. They also solicited feedback on leadership, communication, and work-life balance, seeking to gain a holistic understanding of the factors that influenced engagement and retention.

As the survey responses poured in, Sarah and her team delved into the data with enthusiasm, eager to uncover trends and patterns that would guide their next steps.

They found that employees valued transparency and communication—they wanted to feel informed and involved in the decision-making process. They also discovered that opportunities for growth and development were crucial in driving engagement and retention—employees wanted to know that their organization was invested in their professional development and career advancement.

Armed with these insights, Sarah and her team set to work developing strategies to address the areas of improvement identified in the survey. They launched initiatives to improve communication, increase transparency, and provide more opportunities for growth and development, all with the goal of creating a workplace where every employee felt valued, respected, and empowered to succeed.

As they reflected on the impact of the employee surveys, Sarah felt a sense of satisfaction wash over her. This wasn't just about collecting data—it was about using that data to drive positive change and create a workplace where every employee could thrive.

With their commitment to regular employee surveys reaffirmed, Sarah and her team were ready to take the next step in their journey, confident that they were well-equipped to build a team that would drive TechSolutions forward into a future filled with endless possibilities.

Addressing Feedback and Making Improvements

In the heart of TechSolutions' bustling headquarters, Sarah Thompson and her team gathered around a table strewn with feedback forms and survey results, their faces reflecting a mixture of determination and resolve. They were on a mission—to address the feedback gathered from employees and make tangible improvements to enhance the employee experience.

With a commitment to transparency and accountability, they delved into the feedback with enthusiasm, eager to identify areas for improvement and implement meaningful changes.

They started by analyzing the feedback with a critical eye, looking for common themes and patterns that emerged from the responses. Whether it was concerns about communication, suggestions for enhancing career development opportunities, or requests for improvements to the work environment, every piece of feedback was carefully considered and prioritized.

Armed with this insight, Sarah and her team set to work developing action plans to address the areas identified in the feedback. They launched initiatives to improve communication channels, increase transparency around decision-making processes, and provide more opportunities for career advancement and skill-building.

But they didn't stop there. They also sought to involve employees in the process of making improvements, soliciting their input and ideas for solutions to the challenges they faced. Whether it was through focus groups, town hall meetings, or online suggestion boxes, they wanted employees to feel empowered to contribute their perspectives and help shape the future of the organization.

As the improvements were implemented and the impact began to be felt across the organization, Sarah couldn't help but feel a sense of pride wash over her. This wasn't just about checking boxes—it was about creating a workplace where every employee felt heard, valued, and supported in their journey to success.

With their commitment to addressing feedback and making improvements reaffirmed, Sarah and her team were ready to take the next step in their journey, confident that they were well-equipped to build a team that would drive TechSolutions forward into a future filled with endless possibilities.

Tracking and Improving Retention Rates

In the heart of TechSolutions' strategy room, Sarah Thompson and her team gathered around a monitor displaying a spreadsheet filled with employee data, their expressions focused and determined. They were on a mission—to track and improve retention rates, recognizing that the success of the company depended on the ability to retain top talent.

With a commitment to understanding the factors driving employee turnover, they delved into the data with precision and purpose. They analyzed retention rates by department, tenure, and role, looking for patterns and trends that could offer insights into areas for improvement.

As they sifted through the data, they identified several key factors that contributed to employee turnover. Whether it was lack of career advancement opportunities, dissatisfaction with leadership, or issues with work-life balance, every factor was carefully scrutinized and analyzed.

Armed with this insight, Sarah and her team set to work

developing strategies to address the root causes of turnover and improve retention rates across the organization. They launched initiatives to provide more opportunities for career development and advancement, implemented leadership training programs to improve manager effectiveness, and introduced flexible work arrangements to better support employees' work-life balance.

But they didn't stop there. They also sought to create a culture of retention within the organization, one where employees felt valued, respected, and invested in the company's mission and values. They launched employee recognition programs, implemented mentorship and coaching initiatives, and fostered a sense of community and belonging within the organization.

As they tracked the impact of their efforts on retention rates, Sarah couldn't help but feel a sense of satisfaction wash over her. This wasn't just about reducing turnover—it was about creating a workplace where every employee felt empowered to grow, thrive, and succeed.

With their commitment to tracking and improving retention rates reaffirmed, Sarah and her team were ready to take the next step in their journey, confident that they were well-equipped to build a team that would drive TechSolutions forward into a future filled with endless possibilities.

7

Chapter 7: Leadership Development

In the heart of TechSolutions' innovation hub, a new chapter was unfolding—one focused on leadership development. Sarah Thompson, alongside her team of dedicated HR professionals, gathered with a sense of purpose and determination. They understood that the success of TechSolutions relied not only on its innovative technology but also on the caliber of its leadership.

With this realization driving them forward, they embarked on a journey to cultivate a new generation of leaders who would guide TechSolutions into the future. They knew that effective leadership was not just about authority, but about inspiration, guidance, and empowerment.

As they mapped out their plan for leadership development, they considered the skills and qualities that were essential for success in leadership roles. From communication and decision-making to empathy and resilience, they sought to nurture a diverse set of competencies that would enable leaders to navigate the complexities of the modern business landscape.

They also recognized the importance of diversity and inclusion in leadership, understanding that diverse perspectives lead to better decision-making and innovation. They made it a priority to identify and support emerging leaders from underrepresented groups, ensuring that TechSolutions' leadership team reflected the rich tapestry of its workforce.

But leadership development wasn't just about training programs and workshops—it was also about fostering a culture of continuous learning and growth. Sarah and her team encouraged leaders at all levels to seek out new challenges, take risks, and embrace feedback as opportunities for growth.

As they embarked on this journey of leadership development, Sarah couldn't help but feel a sense of excitement and optimism. This wasn't just about developing leaders—it was about shaping the future of TechSolutions, building a team of visionary leaders who would inspire, innovate, and lead with integrity.

With their commitment to leadership development unwavering, Sarah and her team were ready to take the next step in their journey, confident that they were well-equipped to build a team that would drive TechSolutions forward into a future filled with endless possibilities.

Identifying High-Potential Employees

In the heart of TechSolutions' bustling headquarters, Sarah Thompson and her team gathered around a table adorned with stacks of resumes and performance reviews, their faces reflecting a mix of focus and determination. They were embarking on the crucial task of identifying high-potential employees—those individuals whose talent, drive, and potential for leadership set them apart from the rest.

With a keen eye for talent and a commitment to fostering

growth and development, they delved into the data with enthusiasm, eager to uncover the next generation of leaders who would guide TechSolutions into the future.

As they sifted through the resumes and performance reviews, they looked for signs of potential—whether it was demonstrated leadership in past roles, a track record of exceeding expectations, or a hunger for learning and growth. They also sought to identify individuals who embodied the values and culture of TechSolutions, who were committed to driving the company forward and making a positive impact on the world.

But identifying high-potential employees wasn't just about looking at past achievements—it was also about recognizing potential for future growth and success. Sarah and her team looked beyond the surface, considering factors such as adaptability, resilience, and a willingness to take on new challenges, as indicators of leadership potential.

As they narrowed down their list of high-potential employees, Sarah couldn't help but feel a sense of excitement. This wasn't just about identifying talent—it was about investing in the future of TechSolutions, nurturing the next generation of leaders who would inspire, innovate, and drive the company forward.

With their list of high-potential employees finalized, Sarah and her team were ready to take the next step in their journey of leadership development, confident that they were well-equipped to build a team that would shape the future of TechSolutions and propel it to new heights of success.

Designing Leadership Training Programs

In the heart of TechSolutions' innovation hub, Sarah Thompson and her team gathered around a whiteboard covered with colorful sticky notes, their minds buzzing with ideas as they embarked on the task of designing leadership training programs. They understood that developing leaders wasn't just about identifying talent—it was also about providing them with the tools and resources they needed to succeed.

With a commitment to fostering growth and development, they set to work brainstorming ideas for leadership training programs that would equip high-potential employees with the skills and knowledge to excel in their roles.

They started by mapping out the core competencies that were essential for success in leadership roles—communication, decision-making, emotional intelligence, and strategic thinking, to name a few. From there, they developed a curriculum that encompassed a diverse range of topics, designed to challenge and inspire participants to reach their full potential as leaders.

But designing leadership training programs wasn't just about lectures and workshops—it was also about experiential learning and real-world application. Sarah and her team incorporated hands-on exercises, case studies, and simulations into the curriculum, giving participants the opportunity to put their newfound skills into practice in a safe and supportive environment.

They also recognized the importance of mentorship and coaching in leadership development. They paired program participants with experienced leaders within the organization, who would provide guidance, support, and feedback as they navigated their leadership journey.

As they fleshed out the details of the leadership training programs, Sarah couldn't help but feel a sense of excitement and anticipation. This wasn't just about providing training—it was about empowering high-potential employees to step into their leadership roles with confidence, courage, and conviction.

With their leadership training programs finalized, Sarah and her team were ready to take the next step in their journey of leadership development, confident that they were well-equipped to build a team of visionary leaders who would guide TechSolutions into a future filled with endless possibilities.

Succession Planning and Career Paths

In the heart of TechSolutions' strategy room, Sarah Thompson and her team gathered around a large table, charts and diagrams spread out before them, as they delved into the intricacies of succession planning and career paths. They knew that developing leaders wasn't just about the present—it was about preparing for the future, ensuring that TechSolutions had a strong pipeline of talent ready to step into leadership roles when the time came.

With a commitment to strategic foresight and long-term planning, they set to work crafting a succession plan that would identify and groom future leaders within the organization. They analyzed the skills, competencies, and experiences required for key leadership roles, mapping out potential career paths and development opportunities for high-potential employees.

They also considered the importance of diversity and inclusion in succession planning, ensuring that opportunities for advancement were accessible to employees from all backgrounds and walks of life. They made it a priority to identify and support emerging leaders from underrepresented groups, fostering a culture of inclusivity and opportunity within the organization.

But succession planning wasn't just about filling key roles—it was also about empowering employees to take ownership of their own career paths. Sarah and her team developed career development frameworks and tools to help employees identify their strengths, interests, and aspirations, and chart a course for their future growth and development within the organization.

As they discussed the details of the succession plan and career paths, Sarah couldn't help but feel a sense of pride. This wasn't just about planning for the future—it was about investing in the potential of every employee, empowering them to reach their full potential and achieve their dreams.

With their succession plan and career paths finalized, Sarah and her team were ready to take the next step in their journey of leadership development, confident that they were well-equipped to build a team of visionary leaders who would guide TechSolutions into a future filled with endless possibilities.

Coaching and Mentorship Initiatives

In the heart of TechSolutions' collaborative workspace, Sarah Thompson and her team huddled around a whiteboard, markers in hand, as they brainstormed ideas for coaching and mentorship initiatives. They understood that leadership development wasn't just about training programs—it was also about providing personalized support and guidance to help high-potential employees unlock their full potential.

With a commitment to nurturing talent and fostering growth, they set to work designing coaching and mentorship programs that would pair emerging leaders with experienced mentors within the organization.

They started by identifying potential mentors—seasoned leaders with a wealth of knowledge and experience to share. These mentors would serve as trusted advisors, providing guidance, support, and feedback to their mentees as they navigated their leadership journey.

But coaching and mentorship weren't just about imparting wisdom—it was also about fostering meaningful relationships built on trust, respect, and mutual learning. Sarah and her team developed structured frameworks and guidelines to ensure that both mentors and mentees had clear expectations and goals for their partnership.

They also recognized the importance of diversity and inclusion in coaching and mentorship, ensuring that mentees had access to mentors from a variety of backgrounds and perspectives. They made it a priority to pair mentees with mentors who could provide guidance and support tailored to their unique needs and aspirations.

As they fleshed out the details of the coaching and mentorship initiatives, Sarah couldn't help but feel a sense of excitement and anticipation. This wasn't just about pairing people together—it was about building a culture of support and collaboration, where every employee felt valued, empowered, and supported in their journey to leadership.

With their coaching and mentorship initiatives finalized, Sarah and her team were ready to take the next step in their journey of leadership development, confident that they were well-equipped to build a team of visionary leaders who would guide TechSolutions into a future filled with endless possibilities.

Measuring Leadership Program Outcomes

In the heart of TechSolutions' bustling headquarters, Sarah Thompson and her team gathered around a conference table, laptops open and pens poised, as they prepared to measure the outcomes of their leadership development programs. They knew that in order to gauge the effectiveness of their efforts, they needed to track and evaluate the impact of their initiatives on the organization and its employees.

With a commitment to data-driven decision-making, they delved into the metrics with precision and purpose, eager to uncover insights that would inform future strategies and initiatives.

They started by defining clear and measurable objectives for their leadership programs—whether it was increasing employee engagement, improving retention rates, or fostering a culture of innovation and collaboration. From there, they developed a set of key performance indicators (KPIs) to track progress and measure success.

As they analyzed the data, they looked for trends and patterns that would shed light on the impact of their leadership programs. They examined metrics such as employee satisfaction scores, retention rates, and performance ratings, seeking to understand how participation in the programs correlated with positive outcomes for the organization and its employees.

But measuring leadership program outcomes wasn't just about numbers—it was also about gathering qualitative feedback from participants to understand their experiences and perceptions. Sarah and her team conducted surveys, focus groups, and one-on-one interviews to gather insights into the effectiveness of the programs and identify areas for improvement.

As they reviewed the findings, Sarah couldn't help but feel a sense of satisfaction. This wasn't just about collecting data—it was about using that data to drive positive change and create a workplace where every employee had the opportunity to thrive and succeed.

With their commitment to measuring leadership program outcomes reaffirmed, Sarah and her team were ready to take the next step in their journey of leadership development, confident that they were well-equipped to build a team of visionary leaders who would guide TechSolutions into a future filled with endless possibilities.

Case Study: Cynthia Chen's Journey

In the heart of TechSolutions' vibrant workspace, Sarah Thompson and her team gathered around a projector screen, anticipation filling the air as they prepared to delve into the inspiring case study of Cynthia Chen's journey through the leadership development program.

As the image of Cynthia's smiling face appeared on the screen, Sarah began to narrate her remarkable story—a story of growth, resilience, and transformation.

Cynthia had joined TechSolutions as a junior software engineer, bright-eyed and eager to make her mark on the world. But it wasn't long before her talent and potential caught the attention of her colleagues and mentors, who saw in her the makings of a future leader.

With the support and guidance of her mentor, Cynthia embarked on a journey of self-discovery and growth. She participated in leadership training programs, honing her skills in communication, decision-making, and strategic thinking. She sought out opportunities to take on new challenges, eager to push herself out of her comfort zone and expand her horizons.

But perhaps most importantly, Cynthia embraced the value of mentorship, seeking guidance and support from experienced leaders within the organization who could provide her with insights and advice as she navigated her leadership journey.

As Sarah recounted Cynthia's journey, her teammates listened with rapt attention, inspired by her courage, determination, and resilience in the face of challenges. They saw in Cynthia a shining example of the potential that lay within each and every one of them—a reminder that with dedication, hard work, and the right support, anything was possible.

As the case study drew to a close, Sarah couldn't help but feel a sense of pride. This wasn't just about Cynthia—it was about the countless other employees like her who were on their own journeys of growth and development, each one poised to make a difference in the world.

With Cynthia's journey as a guiding light, Sarah and her team were ready to take the next step in their journey of leadership development, confident that they were well-equipped to build a team of visionary leaders who would guide TechSolutions into a future filled with endless possibilities.

8

Chapter 8: Performance Management

In the heart of TechSolutions' dynamic workspace, a new chapter was unfolding—a chapter focused on performance management. Sarah Thompson and her team gathered around a table, their faces illuminated by the glow of their laptops, as they prepared to embark on the crucial task of optimizing the way performance was measured, evaluated, and rewarded within the organization.

With a commitment to fostering a culture of excellence and accountability, they understood that effective performance management was essential for driving individual and organizational success.

As they delved into the complexities of performance management, they considered the various components that comprised an effective system—from setting clear expectations and goals to providing regular feedback and recognition.

They recognized that performance management wasn't just about evaluating past performance—it was also about setting employees up for success in the future. They developed strategies to align individual goals with organizational objectives, ensuring that every employee understood how their contributions contributed to TechSolutions' overall success.

But perhaps most importantly, they understood the importance of fostering a culture of continuous feedback and improvement. They encouraged managers to provide regular, constructive feedback to their teams, recognizing the value of timely guidance in helping employees reach their full potential.

As they brainstormed ideas and strategies for optimizing performance management, Sarah couldn't help but feel a sense of excitement. This wasn't just about implementing a new system—it was about creating a culture where every employee felt empowered to excel, grow, and succeed.

With their commitment to performance management reaffirmed, Sarah and her team were ready to take the next step in their journey, confident that they were well-equipped to build a team that would drive TechSolutions forward into a future filled with endless possibilities.

Redesigning the Performance Appraisal System

In the heart of TechSolutions' innovation hub, Sarah Thompson and her team huddled around a whiteboard, markers in hand, as they embarked on the monumental task of redesigning the performance appraisal system. They understood that the traditional approach to performance appraisals was outdated and ineffective—it was time for a change.

With a commitment to fostering a culture of transparency, fairness, and growth, they set to work brainstorming ideas for a new system that would better align with TechSolutions' values and objectives.

They started by identifying the shortcomings of the existing system—its focus on past performance, its reliance on subjective evaluations, and its lack of alignment with organizational goals. From there, they developed a vision for a new performance appraisal system—one that would focus on future potential, provide regular feedback, and promote employee development.

They explored innovative approaches to performance assessment, such as 360-degree feedback, peer evaluations, and self-assessments, seeking to capture a more holistic view of employee performance. They also considered the importance of setting clear, measurable goals and objectives, ensuring that every employee understood what was expected of them and how their contributions contributed to the success of the organization.

But redesigning the performance appraisal system wasn't just about changing processes—it was also about changing mindsets. Sarah and her team launched a comprehensive communication and training campaign to educate employees about the new system and its benefits, emphasizing the importance of ongoing feedback, coaching, and development.

As they fleshed out the details of the redesigned performance appraisal system, Sarah couldn't help but feel a sense of excitement and optimism. This wasn't just about implementing a new process—it was about creating a culture where every employee felt valued, supported, and empowered to reach their full potential.

With their commitment to redesigning the performance appraisal system reaffirmed, Sarah and her team were ready to take the next step in their journey of performance management, confident that they were well-equipped to build a team that would drive TechSolutions forward into a future filled with endless possibilities.

Setting Clear Performance Expectations

In the heart of TechSolutions' strategy room, Sarah Thompson and her team gathered around a table strewn with papers and charts, their faces reflecting determination as they tackled the task of setting clear performance expectations. They understood that for performance management to be effective, employees needed to have a clear understanding of what was expected of them.

With a commitment to clarity and transparency, they set to work defining performance expectations for each role within the organization. They started by identifying the key responsibilities and objectives for each position, ensuring that they were aligned with TechSolutions' overall goals and objectives.

They also considered the importance of setting measurable goals and targets, giving employees a clear roadmap for success and providing a basis for evaluating performance. Whether it was sales targets for the sales team, project milestones for the engineering team, or customer satisfaction metrics for the support team, every goal was carefully crafted to be specific, measurable, achievable, relevant, and time-bound (SMART).

But setting clear performance expectations wasn't just about outlining tasks and responsibilities—it was also about fostering a culture of accountability and ownership. Sarah and her team encouraged managers to have regular discussions with their teams about performance expectations, providing guidance, support, and feedback to help employees succeed.

As they finalized the performance expectations for each role,

Sarah couldn't help but feel a sense of satisfaction. This wasn't just about setting goals—it was about empowering employees to take ownership of their work, drive results, and contribute to the success of the organization.

With their commitment to setting clear performance expectations reaffirmed, Sarah and her team were ready to take the next step in their journey of performance management, confident that they were well-equipped to build a team that would drive TechSolutions forward into a future filled with endless possibilities.

Continuous Feedback and Coaching

In the heart of TechSolutions' collaborative workspace, Sarah Thompson and her team gathered around a whiteboard, markers in hand, as they delved into the crucial task of implementing a culture of continuous feedback and coaching. They understood that in order for employees to thrive and grow, they needed regular guidance, support, and recognition.

With a commitment to fostering a culture of learning and development, they set to work brainstorming ideas for how to integrate continuous feedback and coaching into the fabric of the organization.

They started by encouraging managers to have regular one-on-one meetings with their direct reports, providing them with an opportunity to discuss performance, provide feedback, and set goals for the future. They also encouraged peer-to-peer feedback, recognizing the value of insights and perspectives from colleagues who work closely together.

But continuous feedback wasn't just about formal meetings—it was also about creating a culture where feedback was a natural and ongoing part of everyday interactions. Sarah and her team launched training programs to help employees develop their feedback skills, teaching them how to deliver feedback effectively and receive it with an open mind.

They also recognized the importance of coaching in driving employee performance and development. They encouraged managers to take on the role of coach, providing guidance, support, and encouragement to help employees reach their full potential. They also provided resources and tools to help managers develop their coaching skills, ensuring that they had the knowledge and confidence to support their teams effectively.

As they brainstormed ideas and strategies for integrating continuous feedback and coaching into the organization, Sarah couldn't help but feel a sense of excitement. This wasn't just about implementing a new process—it was about creating a culture where every employee felt valued, supported, and empowered to succeed.

With their commitment to continuous feedback and coaching reaffirmed, Sarah and her team were ready to take the next step in their journey of performance management, confident that they were well-equipped to build a team that would drive TechSolutions forward into a future filled with endless possibilities.

Linking Performance to Rewards and Recognition

In the heart of TechSolutions' strategy room, Sarah Thompson and her team gathered around a table, their faces illuminated by the soft glow of their laptops, as they tackled the important task of linking performance to rewards and recognition. They understood that for performance management to be truly effective, employees needed to see a direct correlation between their efforts and the recognition and rewards they received.

With a commitment to fairness and transparency, they set to work brainstorming ideas for how to align performance with rewards and recognition in a way that would motivate and inspire employees to perform at their best.

They started by revisiting the organization's reward and recognition framework, ensuring that it was aligned with TechSolutions' values and objectives. They explored different types of rewards and recognition, from monetary bonuses and promotions to non-monetary incentives such as extra vacation days or public recognition.

But linking performance to rewards and recognition wasn't just about tangible rewards—it was also about creating a culture where recognition was a natural and ongoing part of everyday interactions. Sarah and her team encouraged managers to recognize and celebrate their employees' achievements regularly, whether it was through a simple thank you email or a public shoutout in a team meeting.

They also recognized the importance of fairness and equity in rewards and recognition, ensuring that high performers were appropriately rewarded for their efforts while also providing opportunities for growth and development to employees who may be struggling.

As they brainstormed ideas and strategies for linking performance to rewards and recognition, Sarah couldn't help but feel a sense of satisfaction. This wasn't just about implementing a new process—it was about creating a culture where every employee felt valued, appreciated, and motivated to perform at their best.

With their commitment to linking performance to rewards and recognition reaffirmed, Sarah and her team were ready to take the next step in their journey of performance management, confident that they were well-equipped to build a team that would drive TechSolutions forward into a future filled with endless possibilities.

Addressing Underperformance

In the heart of TechSolutions' bustling headquarters, Sarah Thompson and her team gathered around a table, their expressions serious as they confronted the challenging task of addressing underperformance within the organization. They understood that while fostering a culture of recognition and development was important, it was equally crucial to address instances where employees were not meeting expectations.

With a commitment to fairness and compassion, they set to work brainstorming ideas for how to address underperformance in a way that would support employees in improving their performance while also upholding the standards of the organization.

They started by identifying the root causes of underperformance, whether it was lack of skills or training, unclear expectations, or personal challenges outside of work. They recognized that each situation was unique and required a tailored approach to address effectively.

They explored different strategies for addressing underperformance, from providing additional training and support to setting clear performance improvement plans with measurable goals and timelines. They also considered the importance of open and honest communication, ensuring that employees understood where they were falling short and what steps they needed to take to improve.

But addressing underperformance wasn't just about holding employees accountable—it was also about providing them with the support and resources they needed to succeed. Sarah and her team launched initiatives to provide coaching, mentoring, and additional training to employees who were struggling, ensuring that they had the tools and support they needed to reach their full potential.

As they brainstormed ideas and strategies for addressing underperformance, Sarah couldn't help but feel a sense of empathy for the employees who were struggling. This wasn't just about enforcing rules—it was about helping people overcome obstacles and achieve their goals.

With their commitment to addressing underperformance reaffirmed, Sarah and her team were ready to take the next step in their journey of performance management, confident that they were well-equipped to build a team that would drive TechSolutions forward into a future filled with endless possibilities.

Metrics for Evaluating Performance Management

In the heart of TechSolutions' strategy room, Sarah Thompson and her team gathered around a whiteboard, markers poised, as they delved into the critical task of defining metrics for evaluating the effectiveness of their performance management efforts. They understood that in order to drive continuous improvement, they needed to track and measure the impact of their initiatives on the organization and its employees.

With a commitment to data-driven decision-making, they set

to work brainstorming ideas for metrics that would provide insight into the effectiveness of their performance management processes.

They started by identifying key performance indicators (KPIs) that aligned with TechSolutions' goals and objectives. These included metrics such as employee engagement scores, turnover rates, productivity levels, and performance ratings.

But they also recognized the importance of qualitative feedback in evaluating performance management. They launched surveys and focus groups to gather insights from employees about their experiences with performance management, seeking to understand what was working well and where there was room for improvement.

As they brainstormed ideas and strategies for evaluating performance management, Sarah couldn't help but feel a sense of excitement. This wasn't just about collecting data—it was about using that data to drive positive change and create a workplace where every employee had the opportunity to thrive and succeed.

With their commitment to metrics for evaluating performance management reaffirmed, Sarah and her team were ready to take the next step in their journey, confident that they were well-equipped to build a team that would drive TechSolutions forward into a future filled with endless possibilities.

9

Chapter 9: Learning and Development

In the heart of TechSolutions' innovative workspace, Sarah Thompson and her team gathered around a table, their faces illuminated by the soft glow of their laptops, as they embarked on the exciting journey of learning and development. They understood that in order to stay ahead in a rapidly evolving industry, they needed to invest in the continuous growth and development of their employees.

With a commitment to lifelong learning and growth, they set to work brainstorming ideas for how to create a culture where learning was not just encouraged but celebrated.

They started by identifying the skills and competencies that were critical for success in their industry—whether it was technical skills like coding and data analysis, or soft skills like communication and leadership. From there, they developed a comprehensive learning and development strategy that encompassed a diverse range of learning opportunities, from formal training programs to on-the-job learning experiences.

But learning and development wasn't just about acquiring new skills—it was also about fostering a culture of curiosity, creativity, and innovation. Sarah and her team encouraged employees to take risks, try new things, and embrace failure as an opportunity for growth. They launched initiatives such as innovation challenges and hackathons, providing employees with opportunities to explore new ideas and collaborate with colleagues from across the organization.

As they brainstormed ideas and strategies for learning and development, Sarah couldn't help but feel a sense of excitement. This wasn't just about building skills—it was about building a community of lifelong learners who were passionate about pushing boundaries, challenging the status quo, and driving innovation.

With their commitment to learning and development reaffirmed, Sarah and her team were ready to take the next step in their journey, confident that they were well-equipped to build a team that would drive TechSolutions forward into a future filled with endless possibilities.

Assessing Training Needs

In the heart of TechSolutions' dynamic workspace, Sarah Thompson and her team gathered around a whiteboard, markers in hand, as they embarked on the crucial task of assessing training needs within the organization. They understood that in order to design effective learning and development programs, they first needed to understand the skills gaps and development areas that existed among their employees.

With a commitment to personalized growth and development, they set to work brainstorming ideas for how to assess training needs in a way that was comprehensive and meaningful.

They started by conducting skills assessments and surveys to gather insights into the strengths and weaknesses of their employees. They asked questions about current skill levels, desired areas of growth, and preferences for learning modalities, seeking to understand the unique needs and preferences of each individual.

But assessing training needs wasn't just about gathering data—it was also about fostering open and honest conversations with employees about their career goals and aspirations. Sarah and her team launched initiatives such as career development workshops and one-on-one coaching sessions, providing employees with opportunities to reflect on their career paths and identify areas for growth and development.

As they brainstormed ideas and strategies for assessing training needs, Sarah couldn't help but feel a sense of excitement. This wasn't just about identifying skills gaps—it was about empowering employees to take ownership of their own learning journey, and providing them with the support and resources they needed to succeed.

With their commitment to assessing training needs reaffirmed, Sarah and her team were ready to take the next step in their journey of learning and development, confident that they were well-equipped to build a team that would drive TechSolutions forward into a future filled with endless possibilities.

Designing Effective L&D Programs

In the heart of TechSolutions' vibrant workspace, Sarah Thompson and her team huddled around a table, their minds buzzing with excitement as they delved into the task of designing effective learning and development (L&D) programs. They understood that in order to address the diverse learning needs of their employees, they needed to create programs that were engaging, relevant, and impactful.

With a commitment to innovation and excellence, they set to work brainstorming ideas for how to design L&D programs that would drive growth and development across the organization.

They started by identifying the key objectives of their L&D programs—whether it was upskilling employees in emerging technologies, fostering leadership capabilities, or promoting diversity and inclusion. From there, they developed a comprehensive curriculum that encompassed a diverse range of topics and learning modalities, from traditional classroom training to online courses, workshops, and peer-to-peer learning initiatives.

But designing effective L&D programs wasn't just about content—it was also about creating a culture where learning was woven into the fabric of everyday work life. Sarah and her team launched initiatives such as lunch and learn sessions, book clubs, and cross-functional projects, providing employees with opportunities to learn from each other and apply their new skills in real-world scenarios.

As they brainstormed ideas and strategies for designing L&D programs, Sarah couldn't help but feel a sense of excitement. This wasn't just about building skills—it was about fostering a culture of continuous learning and growth, where every employee felt empowered to reach their full potential.

With their commitment to designing effective L&D programs reaffirmed, Sarah and her team were ready to take the next step in their journey of learning and development, confident that they were well-equipped to build a team that would drive TechSolutions forward into a future filled with endless possibilities.

Leveraging Technology for Learning

In the heart of TechSolutions' innovative workspace, Sarah Thompson and her team gathered around a projector screen, excitement palpable in the air as they delved into the task of leveraging technology for learning. They understood that in today's digital age, technology had the power to revolutionize the way learning and development initiatives were delivered and consumed.

With a commitment to staying ahead of the curve, they set to work brainstorming ideas for how to harness the potential of technology to enhance the effectiveness and accessibility of their learning programs.

They started by exploring a wide range of digital learning platforms and tools, from e-learning modules and virtual classrooms to mobile apps and gamified learning experiences. They sought out solutions that were user-friendly, interactive, and customizable, ensuring that they could cater to the diverse learning preferences and needs of their employees.

But leveraging technology for learning wasn't just about adopting new tools—it was also about creating a seamless and integrated learning experience that could be accessed anytime, anywhere. Sarah and her team launched initiatives such as a learning management system (LMS) where employees could access a library of on-demand courses, webinars, and resources, as well as virtual reality (VR) simulations that provided immersive learning experiences.

As they brainstormed ideas and strategies for leveraging technology for learning, Sarah couldn't help but feel a sense of excitement. This wasn't just about embracing the latest trends—it was about empowering employees to learn and grow in ways that were engaging, relevant, and accessible.

With their commitment to leveraging technology for learning reaffirmed, Sarah and her team were ready to take the next step in their journey of learning and development, confident that they were well-equipped to build a team that would drive TechSolutions forward into a future filled with endless possibilities.

Encouraging a Culture of Continuous Learning

In the heart of TechSolutions' bustling workspace, Sarah Thompson and her team gathered around a roundtable discussion, their faces illuminated by the warm glow of the room's ambient lighting. They understood that fostering a culture of continuous learning was essential for driving innovation and staying ahead in a rapidly evolving industry.

With a commitment to curiosity and growth, they set to work brainstorming ideas for how to cultivate a culture where learning was not just encouraged but celebrated.

They started by leading by example, demonstrating their own commitment to learning and development through their actions and behaviors. They shared stories of their own learning journeys, highlighting the value of taking risks, seeking out new challenges, and embracing failure as an opportunity for growth.

But encouraging a culture of continuous learning wasn't just about leadership—it was also about empowering employees at all levels of the organization to take ownership of their own learning journey. Sarah and her team launched initiatives such as a learning stipend, where employees were given a budget to spend on courses, conferences, and other learning opportunities of their choice.

They also encouraged employees to share their knowledge and expertise with their colleagues through initiatives such as lunch and learn sessions, brown bag seminars, and knowledge sharing forums.

As they brainstormed ideas and strategies for encouraging a culture of continuous learning, Sarah couldn't help but feel a sense of excitement. This wasn't just about building skills—it was about fostering a community of lifelong learners who were passionate about pushing boundaries, challenging the status quo, and driving innovation.

With their commitment to encouraging a culture of continuous learning reaffirmed, Sarah and her team were ready to take the next step in their journey of learning and development, confident that they were well-equipped to build a team that would drive TechSolutions forward into a future filled with endless possibilities.

Measuring the Impact of L&D Initiatives

In the heart of TechSolutions' vibrant workspace, Sarah Thompson and her team gathered around a conference table, their expressions focused and determined as they tackled the critical task of measuring the impact of their learning and development (L&D) initiatives. They understood that in order to demonstrate the value of their programs and drive continuous improvement, they needed to track and evaluate their effectiveness.

With a commitment to data-driven decision-making, they set to work brainstorming ideas for how to measure the impact of their L&D initiatives in a way that was meaningful and actionable.

They started by identifying key performance indicators (KPIs) that aligned with the objectives of their L&D programs—whether it was employee engagement scores, retention rates, productivity levels, or performance improvements. From there, they developed a comprehensive measurement framework that encompassed both quantitative and qualitative data.

But measuring the impact of L&D initiatives wasn't just about collecting data—it was also about using that data to drive positive change. Sarah and her team launched initiatives such as pre- and post-training assessments to measure changes in knowledge and skills, as well as surveys and focus groups to gather feedback from employees about their learning experiences.

They also conducted return on investment (ROI) analyses to quantify the financial benefits of their L&D initiatives, comparing the costs of training with the resulting improvements in employee performance and organizational outcomes.

As they brainstormed ideas and strategies for measuring the impact of L&D initiatives, Sarah couldn't help but feel a sense of satisfaction. This wasn't just about collecting data—it was about using that data to drive continuous improvement and create a culture where learning was valued and supported.

With their commitment to measuring the impact of L&D initiatives reaffirmed, Sarah and her team were ready to take the next step in their journey of learning and development, confident that they were well-equipped to build a team that would drive TechSolutions forward into a future filled with endless possibilities.

Case Studies of Successful Training Programs

In the heart of TechSolutions' collaborative workspace, Sarah Thompson and her team gathered around a screen, their attention captured by the stories of successful training programs from real organizations and companies. They understood the power of learning from others' experiences, and they sought inspiration from those who had achieved remarkable results in their learning and development endeavors.

With a commitment to continuous improvement, they delved into case studies that showcased innovative approaches to learning and development from organizations around the world.

One such case study was from Google, a company renowned for its commitment to employee development. They learned how Google implemented a program called "Googler-to-Googler," where employees could share their expertise with their colleagues through a series of informal, peer-led workshops. This program not only provided employees with valuable learning opportunities but also fostered a culture of collaboration and knowledge sharing across the organization.

Another inspiring example came from Airbnb, a company known for its unique approach to employee training. They discovered how Airbnb developed a program called "Airbnb University," which offered a wide range of courses designed to develop employees' skills and capabilities in areas such as leadership, communication, and cross-functional collaboration. This program not only helped employees build essential skills for success but also contributed to a strong sense of community and belonging within the organization.

As they delved deeper into these case studies, Sarah and her team couldn't help but feel a sense of excitement and inspiration. These real-world examples demonstrated the transformative power of learning and development when approached with creativity, innovation, and a commitment to excellence.

With their enthusiasm fueled by the success stories of others, Sarah and her team were more determined than ever to continue their journey of learning and development, confident that they were well-equipped to build a team that would drive TechSolutions forward into a future filled with endless possibilities.

10

Chapter 10: Compensation and Benefits

In the heart of TechSolutions' strategy room, Sarah Thompson and her team gathered around a table, their faces reflecting a mixture of anticipation and determination as they prepared to tackle the critical topic of compensation and benefits. They understood that in order to attract, retain, and motivate top talent, they needed to offer competitive compensation packages and benefits that aligned with the needs and preferences of their employees.

With a commitment to fairness and equity, they set to work brainstorming ideas for how to design compensation and benefits programs that would reward employees for their contributions and support their overall well-being.

They started by conducting market research to understand industry benchmarks and trends in compensation and benefits. They analyzed data on salaries, bonuses, and other forms of compensation, as well as the types of benefits that were most valued by employees, from health insurance and retirement plans to flexible work arrangements and professional development opportunities.

But designing compensation and benefits programs wasn't just about offering competitive packages—it was also about creating a culture where employees felt valued, appreciated, and empowered to thrive. Sarah and her team launched initiatives such as employee recognition programs, where employees were celebrated and rewarded for their achievements, as well as wellness programs aimed at promoting physical, mental, and emotional well-being.

As they brainstormed ideas and strategies for compensation and benefits, Sarah couldn't help but feel a sense of responsibility. This wasn't just about numbers—it was about people's livelihoods, their sense of security, and their overall quality of life.

With their commitment to designing fair and competitive compensation and benefits programs reaffirmed, Sarah and her team were ready to take the next step in their journey, confident that they were well-equipped to build a team that would drive TechSolutions forward into a future filled with endless possibilities.

Aligning Compensation with Strategic Goals

In the heart of TechSolutions' dynamic workspace, Sarah Thompson and her team gathered around a whiteboard, markers in hand, as they embarked on the crucial task of aligning compensation with the company's strategic goals. They understood that compensation played a vital role in motivating and incentivizing employees to drive performance and achieve organizational objectives.

With a commitment to fairness and transparency, they set to

work brainstorming ideas for how to design a compensation structure that would reward employees for their contributions to TechSolutions' success.

They started by revisiting the company's strategic goals and objectives, ensuring that they were clearly defined and understood by all employees. From there, they developed a compensation strategy that was closely aligned with these goals, linking individual and team performance to tangible rewards and incentives.

But aligning compensation with strategic goals wasn't just about tying bonuses to performance metrics—it was also about creating a sense of ownership and accountability among employees. Sarah and her team launched initiatives such as profit-sharing programs, where employees had a stake in the company's financial success, as well as stock option plans that rewarded long-term commitment and loyalty.

As they brainstormed ideas and strategies for aligning compensation with strategic goals, Sarah couldn't help but feel a sense of excitement. This wasn't just about numbers—it was about creating a culture where every employee felt empowered to contribute to the company's success and share in its rewards.

With their commitment to aligning compensation with strategic goals reaffirmed, Sarah and her team were ready to take the next step in their journey of designing fair and competitive compensation and benefits programs, confident that they were well-equipped to build a team that would drive TechSolutions forward into a future filled with endless possibilities.

Developing a Competitive Benefits Package

In the heart of TechSolutions' bustling headquarters, Sarah Thompson and her team gathered around a conference table, their laptops open and pens poised, as they embarked on the crucial task of developing a competitive benefits package. They understood that in today's competitive job market, offering attractive benefits was essential for attracting and retaining top talent.

With a commitment to employee well-being and satisfaction, they set to work brainstorming ideas for how to design a benefits package that would meet the diverse needs and preferences of TechSolutions' workforce.

They started by conducting surveys and focus groups to gather insights into the benefits that were most valued by employees. From health insurance and retirement plans to flexible work arrangements and professional development opportunities, they sought to understand which benefits would have the greatest impact on employee satisfaction and engagement.

But developing a competitive benefits package wasn't just about offering a laundry list of perks—it was also about creating a package that was aligned with the company's values and culture. Sarah and her team launched initiatives such as wellness programs aimed at promoting physical, mental, and emotional well-being, as well as family-friendly policies that supported employees in balancing their work and personal lives.

As they brainstormed ideas and strategies for developing a competitive benefits package, Sarah couldn't help but feel a sense of responsibility. This wasn't just about attracting talent—it was about taking care of TechSolutions' most valuable asset: its people.

With their commitment to developing a competitive benefits package reaffirmed, Sarah and her team were ready to take the next step in their journey, confident that they were well-equipped to build a team that would drive TechSolutions forward into a future filled with endless possibilities.

Implementing Pay-for-Performance Systems

In the heart of TechSolutions' collaborative workspace, Sarah Thompson and her team gathered around a whiteboard, their expressions focused and determined as they discussed the implementation of pay-for-performance systems. They understood that linking compensation directly to performance was a powerful way to motivate employees and drive results.

With a commitment to meritocracy and fairness, they set to work brainstorming ideas for how to implement pay-for-performance systems that would reward high performers while also providing opportunities for growth and development to all employees.

They started by defining clear and measurable performance metrics that aligned with TechSolutions' strategic goals and objectives. From there, they developed a performance appraisal process that provided regular feedback and evaluations, allowing employees to track their progress and identify areas for improvement.

But implementing pay-for-performance systems wasn't just about evaluating individual performance—it was also about fostering a culture of collaboration and teamwork. Sarah and her team launched initiatives such as team-based incentives and bonuses, where rewards were tied to collective achievements and outcomes.

As they brainstormed ideas and strategies for implementing pay-for-performance systems, Sarah couldn't help but feel a sense of excitement. This wasn't just about compensation—it was about creating a culture where every employee felt empowered to perform at their best and contribute to the success of the organization.

With their commitment to implementing pay-for-performance systems reaffirmed, Sarah and her team were ready to take the next step in their journey, confident that they were well-equipped to build a team that would drive TechSolutions forward into a future filled with endless possibilities.

Communicating Compensation and Benefits Effectively

In the heart of TechSolutions' vibrant workspace, Sarah Thompson and her team gathered around a conference table, their faces illuminated by the glow of their laptops as they discussed the importance of communicating compensation and benefits effectively. They understood that clear and transparent communication was essential for building trust and engagement among employees.

With a commitment to openness and honesty, they set to work brainstorming ideas for how to effectively communicate the company's compensation and benefits programs to its workforce.

They started by developing a comprehensive communication plan that outlined key messages, channels, and timelines for sharing information about compensation and benefits. From town hall meetings and email newsletters to one-on-one sessions and online portals, they sought to leverage a variety of communication channels to reach employees at all levels of the organization.

But communicating compensation and benefits effectively wasn't just about sharing information—it was also about listening and responding to employees' questions and concerns. Sarah and her team launched initiatives such as feedback sessions and surveys to gather input from employees about their preferences and needs, ensuring that the company's programs were aligned with the needs of its workforce.

As they brainstormed ideas and strategies for communicating compensation and benefits effectively, Sarah couldn't help but feel a sense of responsibility. This wasn't just about disseminating information—it was about empowering employees to make informed decisions about their compensation and benefits and ensuring that they felt valued and supported by the organization.

With their commitment to communicating compensation and benefits effectively reaffirmed, Sarah and her team were ready to take the next step in their journey, confident that they were well-equipped to build a team that would drive TechSolutions forward into a future filled with endless possibilities.

Reviewing and Adjusting Compensation Strategies

In the heart of TechSolutions' strategy room, Sarah Thompson and her team gathered around a large table, their laptops open and pens at the ready as they delved into the crucial task of reviewing and adjusting the company's compensation strategies. They understood that in a rapidly changing business environment, it was essential to regularly evaluate and adapt their compensation programs to remain competitive and aligned with the company's goals.

With a commitment to agility and responsiveness, they set to work brainstorming ideas for how to effectively review and adjust their compensation strategies to meet the evolving needs of their workforce.

They started by analyzing market trends and benchmarking data to ensure that their compensation packages remained competitive in the industry. They examined factors such as salary ranges, bonus structures, and incentive programs, seeking to identify areas where adjustments might be needed to attract and retain top talent.

But reviewing and adjusting compensation strategies wasn't just about keeping up with market trends—it was also about responding to feedback from employees and aligning compensation with the company's values and culture. Sarah and her team launched initiatives such as employee surveys and focus groups to gather input on compensation and benefits, as well as regular check-ins with managers and HR to identify emerging trends and issues.

As they brainstormed ideas and strategies for reviewing and adjusting compensation strategies, Sarah couldn't help but feel a sense of urgency. This wasn't just about numbers—it was about people's livelihoods, their sense of fairness and equity, and their overall satisfaction and engagement with the company.

With their commitment to reviewing and adjusting compensation strategies reaffirmed, Sarah and her team were ready to take the next step in their journey, confident that they were well-equipped to build a team that would drive TechSolutions forward into a future filled with endless possibilities.

Metrics for Compensation and Benefits Success

In the heart of TechSolutions' bustling workspace, Sarah Thompson and her team gathered around a whiteboard, markers in hand, as they delved into the crucial task of defining metrics for compensation and benefits success. They understood that in order to evaluate the effectiveness of their programs and drive continuous improvement, they needed to establish clear and measurable metrics.

With a commitment to data-driven decision-making, they set to work brainstorming ideas for how to identify and track key performance indicators (KPIs) related to compensation and benefits.

They started by defining a set of KPIs that aligned with the company's strategic goals and objectives. These KPIs included metrics such as employee satisfaction with compensation and benefits, retention rates, performance ratings, and the cost of compensation as a percentage of revenue.

But defining metrics for compensation and benefits success wasn't just about collecting data—it was also about using that data to drive positive change. Sarah and her team launched initiatives such as regular reviews of compensation benchmarks and market trends, as well as annual audits of the company's benefits programs to ensure they remained competitive and aligned with employees' needs.

As they brainstormed ideas and strategies for defining metrics for compensation and benefits success, Sarah couldn't help but feel a sense of excitement. This wasn't just about numbers—it was about using data to create a better employee experience and drive organizational success.

With their commitment to defining metrics for compensation and benefits success reaffirmed, Sarah and her team were ready to take the next step in their journey, confident that they were well-equipped to build a team that would drive TechSolutions forward into a future filled with endless possibilities.

11

Chapter 11: Organizational Culture and Change Management

In the heart of TechSolutions' vibrant headquarters, Sarah Thompson stood at the front of a packed conference room, her voice steady and confident as she addressed the company's leadership team. They had gathered to delve into the critical topic of organizational culture and change management—a subject that would shape the company's future success.

With a commitment to fostering a culture of innovation and adaptability, Sarah embarked on a journey to explore the fundamental principles that underpinned TechSolutions' identity and the strategies needed to navigate change effectively.

As she delved into the complexities of organizational culture, Sarah highlighted the importance of cultivating an environment where employees felt empowered to challenge the status quo, embrace new ideas, and collaborate across teams to drive innovation.

But she also acknowledged the challenges that came with managing change—the resistance, uncertainty, and fear that often accompanied shifts in strategy or direction. Sarah emphasized the need for strong leadership, clear communication, and empathy in guiding employees through periods of transition.

As the discussion unfolded, Sarah couldn't help but feel a sense of optimism. This wasn't just about managing change—it was about creating a culture where every employee felt valued, supported, and inspired to bring their best selves to work each day.

With their commitment to organizational culture and change management reaffirmed, Sarah and her team were ready to embark on the next phase of their journey, confident that they had the tools and strategies needed to build a company that would thrive in an ever-changing world.

Defining the Desired Organizational Culture

In the heart of TechSolutions' bustling conference room, Sarah Thompson stood before a large whiteboard, marker in hand, as she led the company's leadership team through the process of defining the desired organizational culture. They understood that culture was the heartbeat of the organization—an intangible force that shaped every aspect of their work and interactions.

With a commitment to clarity and alignment, Sarah guided the team through a series of exercises aimed at uncovering the core values, beliefs, and behaviors that would define TechSolutions' culture.

Together, they explored questions such as: What kind of company did they aspire to be? What values were non-negotiable? How did they want employees to feel when they walked through the doors each morning?

As the discussion unfolded, a clear picture began to emerge—a culture characterized by innovation, collaboration, and a relentless pursuit of excellence. They envisioned a workplace where employees felt empowered to take risks, challenge the status quo, and push the boundaries of what was possible.

But defining the desired organizational culture wasn't just about articulating lofty ideals—it was also about translating those ideals into tangible actions and behaviors. Sarah and her team discussed strategies for embedding the desired culture into every aspect of the organization, from hiring and onboarding to performance management and leadership development.

As they brainstormed ideas and strategies for defining the desired organizational culture, Sarah couldn't help but feel a sense of excitement. This wasn't just about creating a workplace—it was about building a community, a family, a home where every employee felt valued, supported, and inspired to do their best work.

With their commitment to defining the desired organizational culture reaffirmed, Sarah and her team were ready to take the next step in their journey, confident that they were laying the foundation for a company that would thrive for years to come.

Assessing the Current Culture and Gaps

In the heart of TechSolutions' bustling conference room, Sarah Thompson and her team sat around a large table, laptops open and pens poised, as they delved into the critical task of assessing the current organizational culture and identifying any gaps that existed between the desired and actual culture.

With a commitment to honesty and introspection, they embarked on a journey of self-reflection, seeking to understand the strengths and weaknesses of TechSolutions' culture and how it aligned with their aspirations.

They started by gathering feedback from employees at all levels of the organization, through surveys, focus groups, and one-on-one interviews. They asked probing questions about the values, norms, and behaviors that defined the company's culture, as well as any areas where employees felt there was room for improvement.

As the feedback poured in, patterns began to emerge—strengths such as a strong sense of camaraderie and a commitment to excellence, but also areas of concern, such as a lack of diversity and inclusion and a tendency towards siloed thinking.

But assessing the current culture and gaps wasn't just about identifying problems—it was also about uncovering opportunities for growth and transformation. Sarah and her team engaged in open and honest discussions about the findings, exploring strategies for addressing the gaps and building a culture that reflected their values and aspirations.

As they brainstormed ideas and strategies for assessing the current culture and gaps, Sarah couldn't help but feel a sense of optimism. This wasn't just about identifying problems—it was about creating a roadmap for change, a blueprint for building a stronger, more resilient organization.

With their commitment to assessing the current culture and gaps reaffirmed, Sarah and her team were ready to take the next step in their journey, confident that they were laying the groundwork for a culture that would drive TechSolutions forward into a future filled with endless possibilities.

Strategies for Cultural Transformation

In the heart of TechSolutions' vibrant headquarters, Sarah Thompson stood before a whiteboard adorned with colorful markers, her eyes alight with determination as she led the company's leadership team through a discussion on strategies for cultural transformation. They understood that changing an organization's culture was no small feat—it required vision, commitment, and a willingness to embrace change.

With a commitment to boldness and innovation, they embarked on a journey to explore the strategies and tactics that would drive TechSolutions' cultural transformation forward.

They started by engaging in open and honest dialogue about the changes needed to align the company's culture with its desired state. They discussed the importance of leadership buy-in, employee engagement, and continuous communication in driving cultural change. They also explored the role of rituals, symbols, and stories in shaping organizational identity and fostering a sense of belonging.

But cultural transformation wasn't just about talking—it was also about taking action. Sarah and her team brainstormed ideas for tangible initiatives that would help bring about the desired changes, from leadership development programs and diversity and inclusion initiatives to redesigning workspaces and implementing new rituals and ceremonies.

As they delved deeper into the strategies for cultural transformation, Sarah couldn't help but feel a sense of excitement. This wasn't just about changing the way things were done—it was about shaping the future of TechSolutions, creating a culture where every employee felt valued, empowered, and inspired to do their best work.

With their commitment to cultural transformation reaffirmed, Sarah and her team were ready to embark on the next phase of their journey, confident that they had the vision, the passion, and the determination needed to build a company that would thrive in an ever-changing world.

Managing Resistance to Change

In the heart of TechSolutions' bustling conference room, Sarah Thompson stood before her team, her expression thoughtful yet determined, as she broached the delicate topic of managing resistance to change. She knew that change was never easy—especially when it involved deeply ingrained habits and beliefs.

With a commitment to empathy and understanding, Sarah led the team through a discussion on the common sources of resistance to change and the strategies for addressing them.

Together, they explored the fear of the unknown—the uncertainty and anxiety that often accompanied change. They discussed the importance of providing clear communication, transparency, and support to help employees navigate through periods of transition.

But managing resistance to change wasn't just about addressing fears—it was also about acknowledging the loss and grief that often accompanied change. Sarah and her team discussed the importance of empathy and compassion in supporting employees through the emotional ups and downs of change, as well as providing opportunities for them to express their concerns and feedback.

As they delved deeper into the strategies for managing resistance to change, Sarah couldn't help but feel a sense of empathy. This wasn't just about pushing through resistance—

it was about building trust, fostering resilience, and creating a sense of shared purpose and commitment to the journey ahead.

With their commitment to managing resistance to change reaffirmed, Sarah and her team were ready to take the next step in their journey, confident that they had the tools and strategies needed to navigate the challenges and uncertainties that lay ahead.

Role of Leadership in Driving Cultural Change

In the heart of TechSolutions' dynamic workspace, Sarah Thompson stood before her team, her gaze steady and unwavering, as she emphasized the pivotal role of leadership in driving cultural change. She knew that leadership set the tone for the entire organization—its values, its behaviors, its priorities.

With a commitment to inspiration and empowerment, Sarah led the team through a discussion on the qualities and behaviors that defined effective leadership in times of change.

Together, they explored the importance of vision—the ability to articulate a compelling vision for the future and inspire others to join in its pursuit. They discussed the role of courage—the willingness to take risks, challenge the status quo, and lead by example.

But leadership in driving cultural change wasn't just about vision and courage—it was also about humility and empathy. Sarah and her team discussed the importance of listening to employees, acknowledging their concerns, and involving them in the change process.

As they delved deeper into the role of leadership in driving cultural change, Sarah couldn't help but feel a sense of responsibility. This wasn't just about leading the organization—it was about creating a legacy, a culture that would endure long after they were gone.

With their commitment to leadership in driving cultural change reaffirmed, Sarah and her team were ready to take the next step in their journey, confident that they had the vision, the courage, and the empathy needed to lead TechSolutions into a future filled with endless possibilities.

Sustaining Cultural Improvements

In the heart of TechSolutions' bustling headquarters, Sarah Thompson stood before her team, her demeanor resolute and determined, as she delved into the critical topic of sustaining cultural improvements. She knew that change wasn't a one-time event—it was an ongoing journey that required dedication, perseverance, and continuous effort.

With a commitment to resilience and adaptability, Sarah led the team through a discussion on the strategies and tactics needed to ensure that the cultural improvements they had worked so hard to achieve would endure over time.

Together, they explored the importance of embedding cultural values into every aspect of the organization—from hiring and onboarding to performance management and leadership development. They discussed the role of rituals and ceremonies in reinforcing cultural norms and fostering a sense of belonging and identity.

But sustaining cultural improvements wasn't just about rituals and ceremonies—it was also about creating systems and structures that supported the desired culture. Sarah and her team discussed the importance of aligning policies, processes, and incentives with the company's values and aspirations, as well as providing ongoing training and development to reinforce desired behaviors.

As they delved deeper into the strategies for sustaining cultural improvements, Sarah couldn't help but feel a sense of determination. This wasn't just about making temporary changes—it was about building a culture that would stand the test of time, a culture that would continue to evolve and grow long into the future.

With their commitment to sustaining cultural improvements reaffirmed, Sarah and her team were ready to take the next step in their journey, confident that they had the resilience, the dedication, and the vision needed to build a company that would thrive for years to come.

12

Chapter 12: Diversity and Inclusion

In the heart of TechSolutions' vibrant workspace, Sarah Thompson stood before a diverse group of employees, her voice filled with passion and conviction as she began to discuss the importance of diversity and inclusion. She knew that in today's global marketplace, diversity wasn't just a buzzword—it was a business imperative.

With a commitment to equity and belonging, Sarah led the team through a discussion on the value of diversity in driving innovation, creativity, and growth. She emphasized the importance of creating an environment where every employee felt valued, respected, and empowered to bring their authentic selves to work.

Together, they explored the various dimensions of diversity—race, gender, ethnicity, sexual orientation, disability, and more—and the unique perspectives and experiences that each individual brought to the table.

But diversity wasn't just about representation—it was also about inclusion. Sarah and her team discussed the importance of creating inclusive policies, practices, and culture that ensured equal opportunities for all employees to succeed and thrive.

As they delved deeper into the topic of diversity and inclusion, Sarah couldn't help but feel a sense of urgency. This wasn't just about doing what was right—it was about doing what was necessary to build a company that reflected the rich tapestry of humanity.

With their commitment to diversity and inclusion reaffirmed, Sarah and her team were ready to take the next step in their journey, confident that they had the passion, the dedication, and the vision needed to create a workplace where everyone felt welcome, valued, and respected.

Importance of Diversity and Inclusion in SHRM

In the heart of TechSolutions' collaborative workspace, Sarah Thompson stood before her team, her voice resonating with passion and purpose as she delved into the importance of diversity and inclusion in strategic human resource management (SHRM). She knew that diversity and inclusion weren't just buzzwords—they were essential components of building a thriving and innovative organization.

With a commitment to equity and fairness, Sarah led the team through a discussion on the profound impact that diversity and inclusion had on every aspect of SHRM. They explored how diverse perspectives and experiences could lead to more creative problem-solving, better decision-making, and increased employee engagement and satisfaction.

Together, they examined the role of SHRM in promoting diversity and inclusion through initiatives such as diverse hiring practices, inclusive leadership development programs, and unconscious bias training. They discussed the importance of creating a culture where everyone felt valued, respected, and empowered to contribute their unique talents and perspectives.

But diversity and inclusion in SHRM weren't just about ticking boxes—they were about creating real change. Sarah and her team brainstormed ideas for how to embed diversity and inclusion into every aspect of the organization's HR policies, practices, and processes, from recruitment and retention to performance management and succession planning.

As they delved deeper into the importance of diversity and inclusion in SHRM, Sarah couldn't help but feel a sense of purpose. This wasn't just about HR—it was about creating a workplace where everyone had an equal opportunity to succeed and thrive.

With their commitment to diversity and inclusion in SHRM reaffirmed, Sarah and her team were ready to take the next step in their journey, confident that they had the passion, the dedication, and the vision needed to build a truly inclusive organization.

Developing a D&I Strategy

In the heart of TechSolutions' vibrant workspace, Sarah Thompson stood before her team, her expression focused and determined as she delved into the process of developing a diversity and inclusion (D&I) strategy. She knew that creating a truly inclusive organization required more than just good intentions—it required a well-thought-out plan of action.

With a commitment to equity and belonging, Sarah led the team through a discussion on the key components of a D&I strategy. They explored how to assess the current state of diversity and inclusion within the organization, identify areas for improvement, and set clear and measurable goals for progress.

Together, they brainstormed ideas for how to embed diversity and inclusion into every aspect of the organization's culture and operations. They discussed the importance of leadership buy-in, employee engagement, and accountability in driving meaningful change.

But developing a D&I strategy wasn't just about policies and procedures—it was also about fostering a culture of openness, respect, and empathy. Sarah and her team discussed the importance of creating opportunities for dialogue and learning, as well as providing support and resources to employees from underrepresented groups.

As they delved deeper into the process of developing a D&I strategy, Sarah couldn't help but feel a sense of optimism. This wasn't just about creating a plan—it was about laying the foundation for a more inclusive and equitable organization, one where every employee felt valued, respected, and empowered to succeed.

With their commitment to developing a D&I strategy reaffirmed, Sarah and her team were ready to take the next step in their journey, confident that they had the vision, the passion, and the determination needed to build a workplace where everyone could thrive.

Implementing Inclusive Hiring Practices

In the heart of TechSolutions' bustling conference room, Sarah Thompson stood before her team, her voice filled with conviction as she delved into the importance of implementing inclusive hiring practices. She knew that building a diverse and inclusive workforce started with the hiring process—the gateway to bringing new perspectives and experiences into the organization.

With a commitment to equity and fairness, Sarah led the team through a discussion on the key elements of inclusive hiring practices. They explored strategies for attracting a diverse pool of candidates, eliminating bias from job descriptions and selection criteria, and ensuring that every candidate had an equal opportunity to succeed.

Together, they brainstormed ideas for how to embed inclusivity into every stage of the hiring process. They discussed the importance of diversifying recruitment channels, providing unconscious bias training for hiring managers, and implementing structured interview processes to ensure fairness and consistency.

But implementing inclusive hiring practices wasn't just about ticking boxes—it was about creating real opportunities for underrepresented groups to succeed. Sarah and her team discussed the importance of building relationships with diverse communities, providing mentorship and support for candidates from underrepresented backgrounds, and holding themselves accountable for progress.

As they delved deeper into the process of implementing inclusive hiring practices, Sarah couldn't help but feel a sense of urgency. This wasn't just about filling job openings—it was about building a workforce that reflected the rich tapestry of humanity, one where every employee felt valued, respected, and empowered to bring their authentic selves to work.

With their commitment to implementing inclusive hiring practices reaffirmed, Sarah and her team were ready to take the next step in their journey, confident that they had the vision, the passion, and the determination needed to build a truly inclusive organization.

Promoting a Culture of Belonging

In the heart of TechSolutions' vibrant workspace, Sarah Thompson stood before her team, her demeanor warm and welcoming as she delved into the importance of promoting a culture of belonging. She knew that diversity and inclusion weren't just about numbers—they were about creating an environment where every employee felt valued, respected, and empowered to be their authentic selves.

With a commitment to empathy and understanding, Sarah led the team through a discussion on the key elements of a culture of belonging. They explored strategies for fostering inclusion, building trust, and creating a sense of community within the organization.

Together, they brainstormed ideas for how to make TechSolutions a place where every employee felt like they truly belonged. They discussed the importance of celebrating diversity, creating opportunities for connection and collaboration, and providing support and resources for employees from underrepresented backgrounds.

But promoting a culture of belonging wasn't just about grand gestures—it was about everyday actions and interactions. Sarah and her team discussed the importance of microaffirmations—small, everyday acts of kindness and inclusion that helped make people feel seen, heard, and valued.

As they delved deeper into the process of promoting a culture of belonging, Sarah couldn't help but feel a sense of optimism.

This wasn't just about changing policies or procedures—it was about changing hearts and minds, creating a workplace where every employee felt like they truly belonged.

With their commitment to promoting a culture of belonging reaffirmed, Sarah and her team were ready to take the next step in their journey, confident that they had the vision, the passion, and the determination needed to build a workplace where everyone could thrive.

Measuring the Impact of D&I Initiatives

In the heart of TechSolutions' bustling conference room, Sarah Thompson stood before her team, her gaze focused and determined as she delved into the importance of measuring the impact of diversity and inclusion (D&I) initiatives. She knew that in order to drive meaningful change, they needed to be able to track their progress and hold themselves accountable for results.

With a commitment to transparency and accountability, Sarah led the team through a discussion on the key metrics and indicators for assessing the impact of D&I initiatives. They explored strategies for collecting data on diversity and inclusion across various aspects of the organization, from recruitment and hiring to employee retention and advancement.

Together, they brainstormed ideas for how to analyze and interpret the data, identifying trends, patterns, and areas for improvement. They discussed the importance of setting clear and measurable goals for D&I initiatives, as well as regularly tracking and reporting progress to senior leadership and stakeholders.

But measuring the impact of D&I initiatives wasn't just

about numbers—it was about stories. Sarah and her team discussed the importance of collecting qualitative feedback from employees, capturing their experiences and perceptions of diversity and inclusion within the organization.

As they delved deeper into the process of measuring the impact of D&I initiatives, Sarah couldn't help but feel a sense of purpose. This wasn't just about collecting data—it was about using that data to drive meaningful change, to create a workplace where every employee felt valued, respected, and empowered to succeed.

With their commitment to measuring the impact of D&I initiatives reaffirmed, Sarah and her team were ready to take the next step in their journey, confident that they had the tools, the knowledge, and the determination needed to build a truly inclusive organization.

Case Studies of Successful D&I Programs

In the heart of TechSolutions' collaborative workspace, Sarah Thompson stood before her team, a stack of case studies in hand, ready to share real-world examples of successful diversity and inclusion (D&I) programs. She knew that learning from the experiences of other organizations could provide valuable insights and inspiration for their own journey.

With a commitment to learning and growth, Sarah led the team through a series of case studies, highlighting the innovative approaches and impactful outcomes of D&I initiatives implemented by renowned companies.

First, she shared the story of **Salesforce**, a global leader in customer relationship management. Salesforce had implemented a comprehensive D&I program focused on increasing representation of women and underrepresented minorities in leadership positions. Through initiatives such as unconscious bias training, mentoring programs, and inclusive leadership development, Salesforce had successfully increased diversity at all levels of the organization, leading to improved business performance and employee satisfaction.

Next, Sarah discussed the example of **Google**, a technology giant known for its commitment to diversity and inclusion. Google had implemented a wide range of D&I initiatives, from employee resource groups and diversity training to targeted recruiting efforts and inclusive product design. By embedding diversity and inclusion into every aspect of its culture and operations, Google had created a workplace where employees felt valued, respected, and empowered to bring their authentic selves to work, leading to increased innovation and employee engagement.

Finally, Sarah shared the inspiring story of **Accenture**, a global professional services company that had made diversity and inclusion a strategic priority. Accenture had implemented a bold D&I strategy focused on creating a culture of belonging, where every employee felt like they truly belonged. Through initiatives such as diversity training, flexible work arrangements, and leadership development programs, Accenture had successfully fostered a culture of inclusion that drove business results and strengthened its competitive advantage in the marketplace.

As they delved deeper into the case studies of successful D&I programs, Sarah couldn't help but feel a sense of excitement. This wasn't just about learning from others—it was about drawing inspiration and insights that would help propel TechSolutions forward on its own journey toward diversity and inclusion.

With their commitment to diversity and inclusion strengthened by the lessons learned from these case studies, Sarah and her team were ready to take the next step in their journey, confident that they had the knowledge, the passion, and the determination needed to build a truly inclusive organization.

13

Chapter 13: Technology and HR Analytics

In the heart of TechSolutions' innovation hub, Sarah Thompson stood before her team, her eyes sparkling with excitement as she introduced the next frontier in strategic human resource management: technology and HR analytics. She knew that harnessing the power of technology and data analytics could revolutionize the way they approached HR, driving insights, efficiency, and impact like never before.

With a commitment to innovation and progress, Sarah led the team through a journey into the world of HR technology and analytics. They explored cutting-edge tools and platforms that could streamline HR processes, automate repetitive tasks, and provide valuable insights into workforce trends and dynamics.

Together, they delved into the potential of artificial intelligence and machine learning to revolutionize recruitment, talent management, and employee engagement. They discussed the role of predictive analytics in forecasting future workforce needs, identifying potential risks, and optimizing decision-making.

But technology and HR analytics weren't just about fancy tools and algorithms—they were about leveraging data to drive meaningful outcomes for the organization and its employees. Sarah and her team discussed the importance of data privacy and ethics in HR analytics, as well as the need for upskilling and reskilling employees to thrive in a digital-first environment.

As they delved deeper into the possibilities of technology and HR analytics, Sarah couldn't help but feel a sense of wonder. This wasn't just about embracing the latest trends—it was about unlocking the full potential of their workforce, driving innovation and growth, and creating a workplace where everyone could thrive.

With their commitment to technology and HR analytics reaffirmed, Sarah and her team were ready to embark on a journey into the future of strategic human resource management, confident that they had the vision, the passion, and the expertise needed to lead TechSolutions to new heights of success.

Leveraging HR Technology for Strategic Insights

In the heart of TechSolutions' state-of-the-art conference room, Sarah Thompson stood before her team, her expression focused and determined as she delved into the potential of leveraging HR technology for strategic insights. She knew that in today's fast-paced business environment, data-driven decision-making was essential for staying ahead of the curve.

With a commitment to innovation and progress, Sarah led the team through a discussion on the transformative power of HR technology. They explored advanced analytics tools and platforms that could help them uncover valuable insights into workforce trends, performance patterns, and talent potential.

Together, they delved into the possibilities of using HR technology to optimize recruitment strategies, identify skill gaps, and improve employee engagement and retention. They discussed how real-time data could empower them to make informed decisions, allocate resources effectively, and drive continuous improvement across the organization.

But leveraging HR technology for strategic insights wasn't just about crunching numbers—it was about gaining a deeper understanding of their most valuable asset: their people. Sarah and her team discussed the importance of combining quantitative data with qualitative insights, such as employee feedback and sentiment analysis, to paint a holistic picture of the workforce.

As they delved deeper into the possibilities of leveraging HR technology for strategic insights, Sarah couldn't help but feel a sense of excitement. This wasn't just about optimizing processes—it was about unlocking the full potential of their workforce, driving innovation, and creating a workplace where everyone could thrive.

With their commitment to leveraging HR technology for strategic insights reaffirmed, Sarah and her team were ready to harness the power of data to propel TechSolutions forward into a future filled with endless possibilities.

Implementing HR Analytics Tools

In the heart of TechSolutions' dynamic workspace, Sarah Thompson stood before her team, her voice filled with determination as she introduced the next phase of their journey:

implementing HR analytics tools. She knew that transitioning from theory to practice would require careful planning, collaboration, and a willingness to embrace change.

With a commitment to innovation and progress, Sarah led the team through a discussion on the practicalities of implementing HR analytics tools. They explored different software options, considering factors such as scalability, ease of use, and integration with existing systems.

Together, they delved into the process of data collection, storage, and analysis, discussing how to ensure data accuracy, security, and compliance with regulations such as GDPR. They brainstormed ideas for building internal capabilities, from hiring data scientists to providing training for existing HR staff.

But implementing HR analytics tools wasn't just about technology—it was about transforming the way they approached HR, from reactive to proactive, from intuitive to data-driven. Sarah and her team discussed the importance of fostering a culture of curiosity and experimentation, encouraging employees to explore and learn from data in their day-to-day work.

As they delved deeper into the process of implementing HR analytics tools, Sarah couldn't help but feel a sense of excitement. This wasn't just about adopting new software—it was about empowering their team to unlock the full potential of data, driving insights, efficiency, and impact across the organization.

With their commitment to implementing HR analytics tools reaffirmed, Sarah and her team were ready to embrace the challenges and opportunities that lay ahead, confident that they had the vision, the passion, and the expertise needed to lead TechSolutions into a future fueled by data and innovation.

Data-Driven Decision Making in HR

In the heart of TechSolutions' innovation hub, Sarah Thompson stood before her team, her eyes gleaming with anticipation as she introduced the concept of data-driven decision making in HR. She knew that embracing data as a guiding force could revolutionize how they approached every aspect of human resource management.

With a commitment to innovation and progress, Sarah led the team through a discussion on the transformative power of data-driven decision making. They explored how leveraging data could enhance their ability to attract top talent, optimize workforce productivity, and foster employee engagement.

Together, they delved into real-life scenarios, examining how data could provide insights into employee performance, identify areas for improvement, and inform strategic initiatives. They discussed the importance of using data to tailor HR interventions to the specific needs and preferences of employees, driving personalized experiences and maximizing impact.

But data-driven decision making in HR wasn't just about numbers—it was about using insights to drive meaningful outcomes for both the organization and its employees. Sarah and her team discussed the importance of combining quantitative data with qualitative insights, such as employee feedback and sentiment analysis, to gain a holistic understanding of the workforce.

As they delved deeper into the concept of data-driven decision making, Sarah couldn't help but feel a sense of excitement. This wasn't just about embracing a new approach—it was about unlocking the full potential of their team, driving innovation, and creating a workplace where everyone could thrive.

With their commitment to data-driven decision making reaffirmed, Sarah and her team were ready to embark on a journey into the future of strategic human resource management, confident that they had the vision, the passion, and the expertise needed to lead TechSolutions to new heights of success.

Predictive Analytics for Workforce Planning

In the heart of TechSolutions' bustling meeting room, Sarah Thompson stood before her team, her voice resonating with excitement as she introduced the concept of predictive analytics for workforce planning. She knew that by harnessing the power of predictive analytics, they could anticipate future workforce needs, identify potential risks, and make strategic decisions with confidence.

With a commitment to innovation and foresight, Sarah led the team through a discussion on the transformative potential of predictive analytics. They explored how historical data, combined with advanced algorithms, could enable them to forecast trends and patterns, from employee turnover to skills gaps.

Together, they delved into real-life examples, examining how predictive analytics had been used by other organizations to optimize workforce planning. They discussed the importance of leveraging data to identify high-potential employees, develop succession plans, and anticipate future talent needs based on business objectives.

But predictive analytics for workforce planning wasn't just about making educated guesses—it was about using data to drive strategic decisions that would shape the future of the organization. Sarah and her team discussed the importance of aligning workforce planning with business goals, ensuring that HR initiatives were directly linked to the organization's overall strategy.

As they delved deeper into the concept of predictive analytics, Sarah couldn't help but feel a sense of anticipation. This wasn't just about embracing a new tool—it was about empowering their team to make more informed decisions, drive innovation, and create a workplace where everyone could thrive.

With their commitment to predictive analytics for workforce planning reaffirmed, Sarah and her team were ready to embark on a journey into the future of strategic human resource management, confident that they had the vision, the passion, and the expertise needed to lead TechSolutions to new heights of success.

Cybersecurity and Data Privacy in HR

In the heart of TechSolutions' secure boardroom, Sarah Thompson stood before her team, her tone serious as she addressed the critical importance of cybersecurity and data privacy in HR. She knew that as they delved deeper into the realm of technology and analytics, safeguarding sensitive employee data would be paramount.

With a commitment to integrity and responsibility, Sarah led the team through a discussion on the potential risks and vulnerabilities associated with HR technology and data analytics. They explored the threat landscape, from data breaches to insider threats, and discussed strategies for mitigating risks and protecting sensitive information.

Together, they delved into the importance of establishing

robust cybersecurity protocols and data privacy policies. They discussed the need for encryption, access controls, and multi-factor authentication to safeguard data against unauthorized access or misuse. They also explored the legal and regulatory requirements governing the collection, storage, and use of employee data, such as GDPR and CCPA.

But cybersecurity and data privacy in HR wasn't just about compliance—it was about earning and maintaining the trust of employees. Sarah and her team discussed the importance of transparency and communication, ensuring that employees understood how their data was being used and protected.

As they delved deeper into the complexities of cybersecurity and data privacy, Sarah couldn't help but feel a sense of urgency. This wasn't just about protecting the organization—it was about safeguarding the privacy and security of every individual whose data they held.

With their commitment to cybersecurity and data privacy reaffirmed, Sarah and her team were ready to implement best practices and protocols that would ensure the integrity and security of TechSolutions' HR data, maintaining the trust and confidence of employees and stakeholders alike.

Future Trends in HR Technology

In the heart of TechSolutions' forward-thinking strategy room, Sarah Thompson stood before her team, her eyes gleaming with anticipation as she delved into the exciting realm of future trends in HR technology. She knew that staying ahead of the curve would be essential for driving innovation and maintaining a competitive edge in the rapidly evolving landscape of human resource management.

With a commitment to innovation and foresight, Sarah led the team through a discussion on the emerging technologies that were poised to reshape the future of HR. They explored the potential of artificial intelligence and machine learning to automate repetitive tasks, personalize employee experiences, and provide actionable insights for decision-making.

Together, they delved into the possibilities of virtual and augmented reality for transforming the way they trained and onboarded employees, creating immersive learning experiences that would drive engagement and retention. They discussed the potential of blockchain technology for securely managing employee credentials and facilitating seamless cross-border talent mobility.

But future trends in HR technology weren't just about adopting the latest gadgets—it was about embracing a mindset of continuous learning and adaptation. Sarah and her team discussed the importance of staying curious and open-minded, exploring new technologies and experimenting with innovative solutions that could unlock new opportunities for growth and development.

As they delved deeper into the possibilities of future trends in HR technology, Sarah couldn't help but feel a sense of excitement. This wasn't just about predicting the future—it was about shaping it, leveraging technology to create a workplace where everyone could thrive.

With their commitment to embracing future trends in HR technology reaffirmed, Sarah and her team were ready to embark on a journey into the unknown, confident that they had the vision, the passion, and the expertise needed to lead TechSolutions into a future filled with endless possibilities.

14

Chapter 14: Measuring Success and Continuous Improvement

In the heart of TechSolutions' dynamic headquarters, Sarah Thompson gathered her team around a table, the atmosphere charged with anticipation as they prepared to delve into the final chapter of their transformative journey. This chapter wasn't just about looking back—it was about measuring success, celebrating achievements, and setting the stage for continuous improvement.

With a sense of pride and accomplishment, Sarah led the team through a reflection on their journey so far. They revisited the goals they had set at the beginning of their strategic HRM initiative, celebrating the milestones they had achieved and the progress they had made in driving positive change throughout the organization.

Together, they delved into the metrics and KPIs they had established to track the impact of their HR initiatives, from employee engagement scores to turnover rates and diversity metrics. They discussed how these metrics had provided valuable insights into the effectiveness of their strategies, guiding decision-making and driving accountability at every level of the organization.

But measuring success wasn't just about ticking boxes—it was about fostering a culture of continuous improvement, where every achievement was seen as a stepping stone to greater heights. Sarah and her team discussed the importance of embracing feedback, learning from both successes and failures, and striving for excellence in everything they did.

As they delved deeper into the process of measuring success and continuous improvement, Sarah couldn't help but feel a sense of gratitude for her team's dedication and hard work. This journey had been challenging, but it had also been incredibly rewarding, bringing them closer together and empowering them to make a real difference in the lives of their colleagues and the success of their organization.

With their commitment to measuring success and continuous improvement reaffirmed, Sarah and her team were ready to embark on the next phase of their journey, confident that they had the resilience, the passion, and the determination needed to overcome any obstacle and achieve even greater success in the future.

Setting Up HR Metrics and Dashboards

In the vibrant heart of TechSolutions' headquarters, Sarah Thompson gathered her team around a sleek, state-of-the-art dashboard display. This moment marked a pivotal juncture in their journey – setting up HR metrics and dashboards to measure success and guide continuous improvement.

With a sense of purpose and determination, Sarah led the team through the process of defining key HR metrics that would serve as the compass for their strategic initiatives. They discussed the importance of aligning these metrics with organizational goals, ensuring that each indicator provided meaningful insights into the health and effectiveness of their HR practices.

Together, they delved into the design of their dashboard, crafting a visually engaging interface that would present HR data in a clear and actionable manner. They discussed the importance of real-time updates and intuitive visualization techniques, empowering stakeholders to track progress and make informed decisions with ease.

But setting up HR metrics and dashboards wasn't just about collecting data – it was about turning that data into actionable insights that would drive meaningful change. Sarah and her team discussed the importance of data literacy and communication, ensuring that everyone within the organization understood the significance of the metrics and how they could contribute to achieving shared goals.

As they delved deeper into the process, Sarah couldn't help but feel a sense of excitement. This dashboard wasn't just a tool – it was a symbol of their commitment to transparency, accountability, and continuous improvement. It would serve as a beacon guiding their journey forward, helping them navigate challenges and seize opportunities along the way.

With their HR metrics and dashboards set up, Sarah and her team were ready to embark on the next phase of their journey, confident that they had the tools and insights needed to measure success and drive TechSolutions towards even greater heights of achievement.

Analyzing HR Data for Insights

In the heart of TechSolutions' bustling analytics lab, Sarah Thompson stood before her team, surrounded by screens displaying a myriad of HR data sets. This moment marked a pivotal step in their journey – analyzing HR data for insights that would drive continuous improvement and innovation.

With a laser focus and determination, Sarah led the team through the process of dissecting the data, mining it for hidden gems of insight that could illuminate their path forward. They discussed the importance of asking the right questions, exploring trends and patterns, and uncovering correlations that could inform strategic decision-making.

Together, they delved into the nuances of the data, exploring employee engagement scores, turnover rates, performance metrics, and more. They discussed how each data point told a story – a story of their organization, its strengths, its challenges, and its opportunities for growth.

But analyzing HR data for insights wasn't just about crunching numbers – it was about gaining a deeper understanding of their most valuable asset: their people. Sarah and her team discussed the importance of empathy and intuition, using data to complement their human-centric approach to leadership and management.

As they delved deeper into the process, Sarah couldn't help but feel a sense of excitement. This wasn't just about uncovering insights – it was about empowering their team to make data-driven decisions that would drive meaningful change and create a workplace where everyone could thrive.

With their commitment to analyzing HR data for insights reaffirmed, Sarah and her team were ready to harness the power of data to unlock new opportunities, drive innovation, and propel TechSolutions towards even greater heights of success.

Continuous Improvement Processes

In the heart of TechSolutions' innovation hub, Sarah Thompson stood before her team, their faces illuminated by the glow of the screens displaying their HR metrics and dashboards. This moment marked the beginning of a new phase in their journey – implementing continuous improvement processes to drive excellence in every aspect of their HR practices.

With a sense of purpose and determination, Sarah led the team through a discussion on the principles of continuous improvement. They explored the concept of Kaizen, the Japanese philosophy of making small, incremental changes over time to achieve continuous improvement.

Together, they delved into the process of identifying areas for improvement within their HR practices, from recruitment and onboarding to performance management and employee engagement. They discussed the importance of soliciting feedback from employees at all levels of the organization, fostering a culture of open communication and collaboration.

But continuous improvement processes weren't just about fixing what was broken – it was about striving for excellence in everything they did. Sarah and her team discussed the importance of setting ambitious yet achievable goals, measuring progress against key performance indicators, and celebrating successes along the way.

As they delved deeper into the process, Sarah couldn't help but feel a sense of optimism. This wasn't just about making incremental changes – it was about fostering a culture of innovation and excellence that would drive TechSolutions towards its vision of becoming a leader in strategic human resource management.

With their commitment to continuous improvement processes reaffirmed, Sarah and her team were ready to embrace the challenges and opportunities that lay ahead, confident that they had the resilience, the passion, and the determination needed to achieve their goals and create a workplace where everyone could thrive.

Regular Review and Adjustment of HR Strategies

In the bustling heart of TechSolutions' strategy room, Sarah Thompson stood before her team, their eyes fixed on her with a shared sense of purpose. This pivotal moment marked the importance of regular review and adjustment of HR strategies—a commitment to staying agile and responsive in the face of change.

With a steady gaze and unwavering determination, Sarah led the team through a discussion on the significance of continuous strategic refinement. They explored the dynamic nature of the business landscape, acknowledging that what worked yesterday might not work tomorrow.

Together, they delved into the process of reviewing their HR strategies, analyzing their effectiveness against established metrics and benchmarks. They discussed the importance of soliciting feedback from stakeholders, from frontline employees to senior executives, to gain diverse perspectives and insights.

But regular review and adjustment of HR strategies wasn't just about reacting to challenges—it was about seizing opportunities for growth and innovation. Sarah and her team discussed the importance of remaining proactive, anticipating trends and disruptions, and adapting their strategies accordingly.

As they delved deeper into the process, Sarah couldn't help but feel a sense of urgency. This wasn't just about staying afloat—it was about leading the charge, driving innovation, and setting new standards of excellence in strategic human resource management.

With their commitment to regular review and adjustment of HR strategies reaffirmed, Sarah and her team were ready to embrace the future with confidence and resilience, knowing that they had the flexibility and adaptability needed to navigate whatever challenges lay ahead.

Communicating Results to Stakeholders

In the bustling headquarters of TechSolutions, Sarah Thompson stood before her team, their faces illuminated by the glow of the screens displaying their latest HR metrics and achievements. This moment marked a crucial step in their journey – communicating results to stakeholders and celebrating their collective successes.

With a confident yet humble demeanor, Sarah led the team through a discussion on the importance of transparent communication. They explored the significance of sharing their progress and achievements with stakeholders, from employees and managers to investors and clients.

Together, they delved into the process of crafting compelling narratives that would resonate with different audiences, highlighting the impact of their HR initiatives on the organization's bottom line, its culture, and its overall success. They discussed the importance of using data to support their stories, providing tangible evidence of their achievements and contributions.

But communicating results to stakeholders wasn't just about sharing good news – it was about building trust, fostering transparency, and inviting collaboration. Sarah and her team discussed the importance of soliciting feedback from stakeholders, listening to their perspectives, and incorporating their input into future decision-making processes.

As they delved deeper into the process, Sarah couldn't help but feel a sense of pride. This wasn't just about showcasing their achievements – it was about recognizing the collective efforts of everyone who had contributed to their success, from the frontline employees to the senior leaders.

With their commitment to transparent communication reaffirmed, Sarah and her team were ready to share their results with the world, confident that they had a compelling story to tell and that their journey was far from over.

Celebrating Successes and Learning from Failures

In the heart of TechSolutions' vibrant office space, Sarah Thompson stood before her team, a twinkle of anticipation in her eyes. This pivotal moment marked the culmination of their journey – celebrating successes and embracing the invaluable lessons learned from failures.

With a warm smile and a sense of camaraderie, Sarah led the team through a reflection on their achievements. They revisited the milestones they had reached, the challenges they had overcome, and the moments of triumph that had defined their journey.

Together, they delved into the significance of celebrating

successes – not just as individual achievements, but as collective victories that reflected the dedication and perseverance of every member of the team. They discussed the importance of acknowledging and appreciating the hard work and contributions of their colleagues, fostering a culture of recognition and appreciation.

But celebrating successes wasn't just about patting themselves on the back – it was about recognizing the lessons learned from failures and setbacks. Sarah and her team discussed the importance of embracing failure as a natural part of the journey, reframing it as an opportunity for growth, learning, and improvement.

As they delved deeper into the process, Sarah couldn't help but feel a sense of gratitude. This journey had been filled with ups and downs, but it had also been incredibly rewarding, bringing them closer together and empowering them to achieve their shared goals.

With their commitment to celebrating successes and learning from failures reaffirmed, Sarah and her team were ready to embark on the next phase of their journey, confident that they had the resilience, the passion, and the determination needed to overcome any obstacle and achieve even greater success in the future.

15

Chapter 15: Reflections and Future Outlook

In the tranquil ambiance of TechSolutions' boardroom, Sarah Thompson stood before her team, the air tinged with a sense of nostalgia and anticipation. This moment marked the final chapter of their transformative journey – a time for reflection on how far they had come and a glimpse into the future that lay ahead.

With a thoughtful expression and a touch of emotion in her voice, Sarah led the team through a journey of introspection. They revisited the challenges they had faced, the triumphs they had celebrated, and the lessons they had learned along the way.

Together, they delved into the significance of their achievements – not just in terms of numbers and metrics, but in terms of the impact they had made on the organization and its people. They discussed the ways in which their strategic HRM initiatives had reshaped the culture of TechSolutions, fostering a workplace where innovation, collaboration, and excellence thrived.

But reflections weren't just about looking back – they were

also about looking forward with hope and determination. Sarah and her team discussed the exciting possibilities that lay ahead – from further refining their HR strategies to embracing new technologies and trends that would shape the future of work.

As they delved deeper into their reflections, Sarah couldn't help but feel a sense of gratitude for her team's unwavering dedication and commitment. This journey had been challenging, but it had also been incredibly rewarding, bringing them closer together and empowering them to make a real difference in the lives of their colleagues and the success of their organization.

With their reflections complete, Sarah and her team turned their gaze towards the future, ready to embrace the opportunities and challenges that lay ahead with optimism, resilience, and a shared sense of purpose. For TechSolutions, the journey was far from over – it was just the beginning of an exciting new chapter filled with endless possibilities.

Reflecting on the Transformation Journey

In the serene atmosphere of TechSolutions' executive lounge, Sarah Thompson stood before her team, the soft glow of the setting sun casting a warm hue over the room. This moment marked a pause in their journey – a time to reflect on the transformation they had undergone, both individually and as an organization.

With a sense of reverence and introspection, Sarah led the team through a journey of self-discovery. They revisited the early days of their transformation journey, recalling the challenges they had faced and the doubts they had overcome. They marveled at the resilience they had shown, the creativity they had unleashed, and the bonds of camaraderie they had forged along the way.

Together, they delved into the significance of their transformation – not just in terms of tangible outcomes, but in terms of personal growth and development. They shared stories of triumph and moments of vulnerability, celebrating the courage it had taken to embrace change and step outside their comfort zones.

But reflecting on the transformation journey wasn't just about looking back – it was also about looking inward with honesty and humility. Sarah and her team discussed the lessons they had learned, the mistakes they had made, and the wisdom they had gained from their experiences. They acknowledged the importance of self-awareness and resilience, recognizing that true transformation began from within.

As they delved deeper into their reflections, Sarah couldn't help but feel a sense of pride. This journey had challenged them in ways they never imagined, but it had also brought out the best in each of them, revealing strengths they never knew they had and instilling a sense of purpose that would guide them in the years to come.

With their reflections complete, Sarah and her team stood united, ready to embrace the future with renewed vigor and determination. For TechSolutions, the transformation journey was far from over – it was a continuous evolution, fueled by passion, perseverance, and an unwavering commitment to excellence.

Lessons Learned from the Case Study

In the hushed ambiance of TechSolutions' strategy room, Sarah Thompson stood before her team, a projector illuminating the screen behind her with the title: "Lessons Learned from the Case Study." This pivotal moment marked a deep dive into the invaluable insights gleaned from their journey—a time to distill wisdom from their experiences and apply it to shape their future endeavors.

With a demeanor of contemplation and reverence, Sarah guided the team through an exploration of the case study. They revisited the pivotal moments, the trials, and the triumphs, dissecting each with a keen eye for lessons learned. They marveled at the resilience they had exhibited, the innovative solutions they had devised, and the collaborative spirit that had propelled them forward.

Together, they delved into the significance of the case study—not merely as a record of their achievements, but as a compendium of wisdom to inform their future actions. They shared anecdotes of overcoming obstacles, navigating uncertainty, and emerging stronger on the other side. They celebrated the power of teamwork, adaptability, and unwavering commitment to their shared vision.

But the lessons learned from the case study weren't just about looking back—it was about looking forward with clarity and purpose. Sarah and her team discussed the importance of applying these insights to future challenges, leveraging their newfound knowledge to drive innovation, and cultivate a culture of continuous improvement.

As they delved deeper into the discussion, Sarah couldn't help but feel a sense of gratitude. This case study wasn't just a testament to their past accomplishments—it was a roadmap for their future success, a reminder of the resilience and ingenuity that had brought them this far.

With their lessons learned from the case study internalized, Sarah and her team stood united, poised to embark on the next chapter of their journey with confidence, wisdom, and an unwavering commitment to excellence. For TechSolutions, the future held boundless possibilities, guided by the invaluable lessons learned from their transformative experience.

Ongoing Challenges and Areas for Improvement

In the quiet confines of TechSolutions' conference room, Sarah Thompson stood before her team, the hum of anticipation filling the air. This moment marked a critical juncture in their journey – a time to confront the ongoing challenges and identify areas for improvement that would shape their path forward.

With a blend of determination and humility, Sarah led the team through a candid discussion on the persistent hurdles they faced. They revisited the roadblocks encountered along their journey, acknowledging that transformation was an ongoing process, not a destination reached.

Together, they delved into the intricacies of their ongoing challenges – from resistance to change to the need for greater diversity and inclusion. They discussed the importance of facing these challenges head-on, recognizing that true growth and innovation stemmed from overcoming adversity.

But the discussion didn't stop at challenges – it extended to areas for improvement, opportunities to refine their strategies and practices to better serve their organization and its people.

Sarah and her team discussed the importance of embracing feedback, fostering a culture of continuous learning and adaptation.

As they delved deeper into the discussion, Sarah couldn't help but feel a surge of determination. These ongoing challenges were not insurmountable obstacles – they were opportunities for growth, catalysts for innovation, and tests of their resilience as a team.

With their commitment to confronting ongoing challenges and embracing areas for improvement reaffirmed, Sarah and her team stood ready to tackle whatever the future held with courage, conviction, and a steadfast dedication to their shared vision of excellence. For TechSolutions, the journey was far from over – it was an ongoing evolution, fueled by a relentless pursuit of progress and a commitment to continuous improvement.

Future Trends in SHRM

In the dimly lit boardroom of TechSolutions, Sarah Thompson stood before her team, the glow of anticipation lighting up the room. This moment marked a pivotal discussion – an exploration of the future trends in SHRM that would shape their strategic direction in the years to come.

With an air of excitement and curiosity, Sarah led the team through a visionary exploration of the evolving landscape of SHRM. They delved into the emerging trends reshaping the world of work, from remote and hybrid models to the rise of AI and automation.

Together, they dissected the implications of these trends on their organization, brainstorming innovative strategies to harness their potential and mitigate their challenges. They discussed the importance of staying ahead of the curve, embracing agility and adaptability as they navigated the ever-changing landscape of SHRM.

But the discussion didn't stop at trends – it extended to opportunities for innovation and growth. Sarah and her team envisioned a future where SHRM was not just a function within the organization, but a strategic partner driving business success and societal impact.

As they delved deeper into the discussion, Sarah couldn't help but feel a sense of excitement. The future of SHRM was brimming with possibilities – opportunities to leverage technology, foster inclusivity, and redefine the way organizations approached talent management.

With their commitment to embracing future trends in SHRM reaffirmed, Sarah and her team stood ready to embark on the next phase of their journey with courage, vision, and a relentless determination to lead the way in shaping the future of work. For TechSolutions, the future was bright – and they were poised to seize it with both hands.

Preparing for the Future Workforce

In the luminous confines of TechSolutions' innovation hub, Sarah Thompson stood before her team, the air crackling with anticipation. This moment marked a crucial discussion – preparing for the future workforce, a journey into the unknown terrain of tomorrow's talent landscape.

With a blend of foresight and determination, Sarah led the team through a visionary exploration of the future workforce. They contemplated the seismic shifts on the horizon – from the gig economy to the rise of Gen Z – and the implications for their organization.

Together, they dissected the skills and competencies that would define success in the future, envisioning a workforce that was agile, adaptable, and digitally savvy. They discussed the importance of nurturing a culture of lifelong learning, empowering employees to thrive in an era of constant change.

But the discussion didn't stop at predictions – it extended to action plans and strategies for success. Sarah and her team brainstormed innovative approaches to talent acquisition, development, and retention, ensuring they were equipped to attract and retain the best and brightest talent in the years to come.

As they delved deeper into the discussion, Sarah couldn't help but feel a surge of excitement. The future workforce held boundless potential – a diverse tapestry of talents, perspectives, and experiences that would drive innovation and propel TechSolutions to new heights of success.

With their commitment to preparing for the future workforce reaffirmed, Sarah and her team stood ready to embrace the challenges and opportunities that lay ahead with courage, resilience, and an unwavering dedication to excellence. For TechSolutions, the future was not a distant dream – it was a reality they were poised to shape and define.

Final Thoughts and Actionable Takeaways

In the tranquil setting of TechSolutions' executive lounge, Sarah Thompson stood before her team, a sense of serenity permeating the room. This moment marked the culmination of their journey – a time for final reflections and actionable takeaways to guide them into the future.

With a heartfelt expression and a touch of nostalgia, Sarah shared her final thoughts with the team. She spoke of the incredible journey they had undertaken together – the challenges they had faced, the triumphs they had celebrated, and the lessons they had learned along the way.

Together, they revisited the core principles that had guided them – from a relentless commitment to excellence to an unwavering dedication to collaboration and innovation. They reflected on the bonds they had forged, the memories they had created, and the legacy they were building together.

But final thoughts weren't just about looking back – they were also about looking forward with hope and determination. Sarah shared actionable takeaways to guide them into the future – reminders to stay agile, embrace change, and never lose sight of their shared vision.

As they absorbed Sarah's final words, the team couldn't help but feel a sense of gratitude. This journey had been transformative in more ways than one – it had brought them together, challenged them to grow, and empowered them to make a real difference in the world.

With their hearts full and their spirits renewed, Sarah and her team stood united, ready to embrace the future with courage, resilience, and an unwavering commitment to their shared values. For TechSolutions, the journey was far from over – it was just the beginning of an exciting new chapter filled with endless possibilities.

About the Author

Goodson Mumba is a multifaceted individual known for his diverse expertise and prolific contributions across various fields. As an infopreneur, Management Consultant, thought leader, and spiritual leader, he has inspired countless individuals through his insightful teachings and impactful writings. Mumba is also an accomplished author, with several notable works to his name, including "Understanding Corporate Worship," "The Years I Spent in a Week," "Management By Harmony," "The CEO's Diary," "Change to Change" and "Creative Thinking for results" His literary works span topics ranging from business management to personal development and spirituality, reflecting his broad range of interests and insights.

With a Master of Business Leadership (MBL) and a Bachelor of Arts in Theology (BTh), Mumba brings a unique blend of business acumen and spiritual wisdom to his work. His educational background is further enriched by a Group Diploma in Management Studies, providing him with a solid foundation in organizational dynamics and leadership principles. Additionally, Mumba holds diplomas in Education Psychology, Leadership and Management Styles, Organizational Behaviour, Financial Accounting, Economic Growth and Development, and Project Management, showcasing his commitment to continuous learning and professional development.

Mumba's expertise extends beyond traditional academic disciplines, encompassing areas such as Neuro-Linguistic Programming (NLP) and Positive Psychology. His diverse skill set is complemented by a range of certifications, including Creative Problem Solving and Decision Making, Life Coaching Fundamentals and Techniques, Professional Life Coaching, and Performance Management System Design. These certifications reflect Mumba's dedication to equipping himself with the tools and knowledge necessary to empower others and drive positive change.

As an author, Mumba's writings reflect his deep understanding of human nature, organizational dynamics, and spiritual principles. His works offer practical insights, actionable strategies, and inspirational guidance for individuals seeking personal growth, professional success, and spiritual fulfillment. Mumba's holistic approach to life and leadership resonates with readers worldwide, making him a respected figure in both the business and spiritual communities.

Overall, Goodson Mumba's diverse background, extensive knowledge, and profound insights make him a sought-after speaker, mentor, and author. His commitment to excellence, lifelong learning, and service to others continues to inspire individuals to unlock their full potential and lead lives of purpose and significance.

Goodson Mumba is renowned for initiating the concept of Management by Harmony, revolutionizing traditional management practices with a focus on balanced and holistic approaches. He has authored two influential books on this subject: "Introduction to Management by Harmony" and its sequel, "Management by Harmony."

Mumba's work has significantly impacted the field, offering innovative strategies for fostering organizational harmony and efficiency. His contributions continue to shape contemporary management theories and practices.

www.ingramcontent.com/pod-product-compliance
Lightning Source LLC
Chambersburg PA
CBHW071829210526
45479CB00001B/55